BECOMING HUMAN

Becoming Human

Embracing Imperfection and Finding Purpose

Dinakara Nagalla

©2025 All Rights Reserved. No portion of this book may be reproduced, stored in a retrieval system, or transmitted in any form or by any means—electronic, mechanical, photocopy, recording, scanning, or other—except for brief quotations in critical reviews or articles without the prior permission of the author.

Published by Game Changer Publishing

Paperback ISBN: 978-1-966659-70-9

Hardcover ISBN: 978-1-966659-71-6

Digital ISBN: 978-1-966659-72-3

NOTE: All proceeds from this book directly fund Saayam's nonprofit initiatives, ensuring that every purchase makes an immediate and meaningful impact on communities in need.

www.GameChangerPublishing.com

DEDICATION

To my **aunt**, **mother, and brothers**—*the backbone of everything I am.* **My aunt**, *a silent* **force of inspiration**, *leading by example, not through words, but through the way she lived her life.* **My mother**, *who never broke, even when life tried to break her. She showed me what love looks like—not in words, not in grand gestures, but in* **quiet sacrifices**. **My brothers**, *the best I never asked for, my* **rocks** *when life got unsteady.*

To my kids—*I wish I could promise you an easy road, but life doesn't work that way. What I can promise is this: I have loved you, every moment, even from a distance. Even in the moments you didn't see me. Even when I failed you. I carry you with me in everything I do, and if nothing else, I hope you see that no matter how many times life knocks you down, you get the hell back up.*

To my friends—*to all, old and new, and to the few who never asked for explanations, who never needed the full story to stand beside me. You inspired me, not through words, but through action. You are my people—the ones who knew me at my worst and still saw something worth believing in. I don't say it enough, but I see you. I will always see you.*

And to you—*yes, you. The one reading this. The one who second-guesses every decision, who feels trapped between what the world expects and what your soul screams for. This book is yours as much as it is mine. Because I've been there.*

I've sat in the silence, drowning in my own thoughts, wondering if I'd ever find a way out. You are not alone.

Life is brutal, beautiful, and absolutely unfair. But if you're still standing, if you're still fighting, then you're already ahead. Keep going.

This is for us—the ones who refuse to break.

READ THIS FIRST

Just to say thanks for buying and reading my book, I would like to give you a free welcome call with me, no strings attached!

Scan the QR Code Here:

BECOMING HUMAN
EMBRACING IMPERFECTION AND FINDING PURPOSE

DINAKARA NAGALLA

FOREWORD
BY QUINTON SMITH, COWBOYS FIT

"But the secret of life is this: we are not human beings; we are human becomings.."

This book isn't just pages filled with words—it's an invitation to step into the unknown parts of your life, push through doubts, face your fears, and embrace whatever comes your way. It's an invitation to be brave enough to find the person you're meant to become.

Dinakara Nagalla does an incredible job of bringing this message to life—not through empty self-help advice, but through real, raw honesty. *Becoming Human* is a journey, a dive into what it really means to live and be a part of the human experience. It makes you ask, "Am I truly following my own dreams, or am I just running a race that someone else set for me?" It makes you look at all the invisible rules we carry—family, culture, society—and decide for yourself what is truly authentic and what you decide to let go.

"Don't waste your time chasing an image of who you think you should be. Instead, be curious about who you are and brave enough to meet who you are becoming."These words really set the tone for what's to come—a journey of unlearning, questioning, and reclaiming your own story.

One of the most powerful parts of this book is how it talks about parenthood. Dinakara doesn't present being a father as something you perfect, but as a constant process of surrendering control. He writes, "As parents, we have the privilege and the opportunity to make peace with our limitations, to break cycles of pain, and to face our own shadows with the power of being present." Parenthood, like life itself, isn't about control—it's about showing up. It's about being present, failing, learning, and trying again.

This book also takes a hard look at our perception of success and failure—how we define them and how they, in turn, shape us. Dinakara reminds us that "Growth doesn't follow a timeline, and transformation isn't bound by age or circumstances. Every failure carves a deeper well for wisdom, every heartbreak teaches you the depth of love, and every uncertainty forces you to find strength you didn't know you had."

Through his own experiences—building businesses, navigating relationships, and dealing with loss—he challenges the idea that success is a final destination. He encourages us to think about what we're really chasing and, more importantly, why.

Reading this book felt like taking a breath of fresh air. It gave me space to pause, reflect, and make sense of some places of my life that brought me shame. If you're looking for perspective and grounding—this book is definitely worth reading.

"This is your life, unfolding, messy, and gloriously unfinished. Don't settle for whispers when you were born to roar. Don't wait for clarity when action will bring it. The world needs your fire, your vision, and your untamed, unpolished truth. It needs your mistakes, your lessons, and your moments of quiet triumph. Be raw. Be bold. Be the voice that cuts through the noise with purpose and presence."

I encourage you to take this journey with Dinakara. You won't regret it.

FOREWORD
BY SIVA SOMAYAJULA, CTO OF ALIVECOR

Dinakar—Dinu, as we called him—has been part of my life since childhood. We grew up together in Tenali, India, sharing classrooms, mischief, and the kind of moments that shape lifelong bonds. He wasn't the kid fighting for the front-row seat or chasing academic ranks, but he carried himself with a quiet confidence that naturally drew people toward him.

I was different—quick with words, sometimes too sharp for my own good. One day on the volleyball court, I made a joke at his expense, expecting laughs. But Dinu wasn't amused. He warned me once, then again. I, of course, didn't stop. And just like that, we ended up in a fight—one I was destined to lose. It wasn't a big brawl, but it was enough to create a distance between us. Months passed without a word. Then one day, it was Dinu who walked up to me and offered a handshake. No drama, no ego—just an understanding that some things aren't worth holding onto. Looking back, that moment wasn't just about our friendship; it was a glimpse of the man he was becoming.

Life took us on different paths, but Dinu remained the kind of person who never let connections fade. Even as we moved to the U.S. nearly three decades ago, he found ways to keep friendships alive, no matter the miles in between. And while most of us followed the predictable path, Dinu did what few dared—he built something from scratch. He launched a software business in aviation, a career that took off. Along the way, he didn't just

FOREWORD

create success for himself—he lifted others, helping friends secure opportunities, visas, and jobs. Many of them still work with him today.

On the surface, he had it all—the dream career, the family, the big house. But life isn't just what people see from the outside. When he called me one afternoon to tell me about his divorce, it caught me off guard. This was Dinu—the man who had always been about loyalty and responsibility—now facing a reality none of us expected. And yet, even in that pain, he never spoke with anger or resentment. He didn't place blame. Instead, he looked inward, questioning himself, his choices, and what it meant to start over.

I met him several times after that, and each time, I saw the shift—his world now revolved around his children. Where work had once been the priority, now it was them. It wasn't an easy road, but it was one he walked with the same quiet strength he had always carried.

Then, he sent me this book.

I read it and saw not just his story, but a reflection of all of us—people navigating ambition, relationships, failures, and the constant battle between impulse and wisdom. This isn't a book filled with easy answers. Dinu doesn't pretend to have life figured out, and that's exactly what makes it worth reading. Instead of offering a step-by-step guide, he lays out his thoughts, his struggles, his way of making sense of it all, and invites you to do the same.

For years, I've seen Dinu lift people up without needing recognition. Now, through *Becoming Human*, he extends that same generosity to his readers. He writes not to teach, but to share—to offer a conversation about the contradictions and complexities that make us who we are.

This book isn't just words on a page. It's a story of resilience, self-awareness, and the courage to face life without illusions. I hope as you turn these pages, you see not just Dinu's journey but glimpses of your own.

Because at the heart of it, that's what this book is about—not perfection, not easy solutions, but the raw, unfiltered experience of being human.

ACKNOWLEDGMENTS

I want to start by thanking my kids—who, from a very young age, had to endure hours of me blabbering about most of the things that ended up in this book. They don't even realize it, but they have been my greatest teachers. Every mistake, every breakthrough, every hard lesson—I learned it first through them.

To my aunt—who always encouraged me, never hesitated to appreciate the smallest good, and never held back when I needed to hear the truth. Her library introduced me to three minds that shook my foundation: Sri Sri, Jiddu Krishnamurti, and Rabindranath Tagore—without whom I may have never started questioning everything.

To my brothers and friends—who stayed through my adult journey, giving me space to experiment, to fail, and to grow. You didn't just stand by; you held my hand when I needed it and stepped back when I needed to figure things out for myself, giving me time to focus on writing this book without distraction.

To my fitness intruder turned pal—what started as a simple correction in form became a space where we unraveled life, purpose, and everything in between. Your constant push—conversation to reflection to action—turned my 468 email drafts into this book. You saw a bigger purpose, not just for those I talk to, but for anyone lost in their own chaos.

To my car buyer turned amazing friend—a transaction became a conversation that never really ended. Your deep regard for me and our talks on mental health gave me the push to go bold.

And finally, to the reader—this book isn't just mine. If even a single sentence resonated with you, then this book belongs to you too. You didn't have to pick it up, but you did. And for that, you have my deepest respect.

CONTENTS

Introduction — xvii

0. The Uncharted Territory of Life — 1
   A Shared Struggle with a Personal Lens
1. The Impulse Within — 5
   Navigating the Tension Between Authenticity and Expectation
2. Quantum Sciences and Karma — 11
   Understanding the Forces That Shape Our Lives
3. Leadership, Legacy, and the Weight of Decisions — 17
   A Harsh Reality Check
4. Navigating Relationships — 23
   The Complex Dance of Connection and Self-Identity
5. The Inner Struggle — 29
   Managing Impulsivity and Finding Balance
6. The Inner Struggle — 35
   Embracing Imperfections and Finding Balance
7. Love, Loss, and the Journey to Finding Connection — 41
   in the Second Half of Life
8. Parenting in the Present — 51
   Navigating Parenthood with Mindfulness and Intention
9. Embracing Self-Compassion — 57
   The Key to Lasting Change
10. Building Resilience — 63
    Navigating Relationships, Setbacks, and the Unpredictable
11. Cultivating Inner Peace — 69
    Navigating the Chaos with Stillness
12. The Power of Gratitude — 75
    Shifting Focus to Abundance
13. Manifesting Intentions — 81
    Turning Thought into Reality
14. Embracing Change — 89
    Navigating Life's Transitions with Grace
15. The Art of Being Present — 95
    Cultivating Mindfulness in Every Moment
16. Integrating the Journey — 101
    Creating a Life of Harmony

17. Embracing Uncertainty 107
Trusting the Unknown
18. Navigating Success and Failure 113
Redefining Achievement
19. The Balance of Solitude and Connection 119
Finding Harmony in Relationships
20. Empathy and Leadership 125
Creating Impact Through Compassion
21. The Journey Continues 131
Embracing Lifelong Growth
22. A Life of Purpose and Presence 137
Conclusion 141

Thank You For Reading My Book! 145

INTRODUCTION
UNRAVELING LIFE'S PROGRAMMING AND THE JOURNEY TO SELF-DISCOVERY

We enter this world with no memory of who we really are, yet we arrive carrying more than we realize and more than we bargained for. From the moment we take our first breath, we are shaped by forces that are far beyond our control. Some say we carry echoes of past lives, while others point to the genetic programming embedded deep within us, traits passed down through generations, impacting our behavior, decisions, and emotions. The past shapes us before we have the capacity to understand it.

As we grow older, this programming is intertwined with the world around us, including our family's expectations, societal norms, and cultural beliefs. We are taught what success should look and feel like, what happiness should and should not be, and how to chase dreams in an ever-evolving world that demands endless achievements.

However, somewhere along the way, we begin to question this notion of life, and that's when whys and why-nots creep in. I don't know if the lucky ones are those who go through this or the people who run through life with a burden that does not give them an opportunity to think about anything.

Are we truly chasing our own ambitions, or are we just running a race set out for us by those who came before? Is the path we walk one of our choosing, or have we been subtly conditioned by the world to fit into a predefined mold? These questions, often drowned out by the noise of life's constant demands, echo in our quiet moments, urging us loudly to dig deeper.

We carry the weight of our ancestry, not just in our DNA but in the values, beliefs, and fears passed down through generations. Genetic programming might make us predisposed to certain behaviors, addictions, or emotions, while cultural conditioning tells us what to do with them. At some point, each of us must confront this. Are we merely products of these unseen forces, or do we have the power to break free and create our own path?

In the Telugu song from the classic film *Sagara Sangamam*, there is a poignant message: "Life is a dance, and it is Eswara's (God's) dance." This reflects the delicate balance between our personal will and the divine forces that shape our lives. As dancers in this grand performance, we sometimes lead with our choices and intentions. At other times, we must follow, surrendering to the rhythm set for us. Each step, whether a leap forward or a stumble backward, shapes where we land. There's no script, just our raw attempts at figuring it out. The imperfections, uncertainties, and moments of stillness all contribute to the richness of our existence.

As we navigate through childhood, adolescence, and adulthood, life tests us at every turn. We face heartbreaks that teach us the fragility of connection, victories that often feel hollow, and a constant pull between our deepest desires and society's expectations. We learn that dreams are not always what they seem and that success can be a double-edged sword. The rat race promises satisfaction, yet more often than not, it leaves us yearning for something more—a deeper sense of purpose, a life that feels authentically our own.

Throughout these journeys, dark thoughts sometimes cloud our path: the fear of failure, the weight of not measuring up, the haunting question of whether we are living our truth or someone else's version of it. We begin to wonder, is this all there is? Are we destined to live out the patterns and programming of our past, or can we forge a new way forward—one driven by our own choices, desires, and sense of fulfillment?

This book is my attempt to answer that question. I've lived through the conflicts we all face—balancing the pursuit of success with the search for happiness, navigating the shadows of past influences, and questioning the legacy we wish to leave behind. It's a journey that has no easy answers, but along the way, I've learned that life isn't about perfection. It's about finding our way through the layers of programming—genetic, societal, and emotional—and emerging with a clearer sense of who we are and what truly matters.

In the end, it's not about escaping the past or denying its influence. It's about learning to live consciously within it, make choices that reflect our true selves, and find peace in the knowledge that we can shape our destinies, no matter what we've inherited.

As we move through this exploration, I will offer my perspective on what I believe is worth pursuing in life. Is it fame, success, or something deeper, something more enduring? Together, we'll untangle the threads of the past, confront the programming that shaped or shapes us, and discover the power to live a life that is truly our own. Together, we'll take what life throws at us—sometimes we're in charge, sometimes we're just hanging on—but either way, we keep moving, figuring it out as we go.

ZERO
THE UNCHARTED TERRITORY OF LIFE
A SHARED STRUGGLE WITH A PERSONAL LENS

Life always unfolds before us like an unmarked map. From the start, we are handed gifts and burdens, expectations and histories, and dreams that aren't entirely our own. We often try to walk in the shoes laid out for us, sometimes with confidence, sometimes with hesitation, often wondering who we're meant to become and if we're on the right path. I've asked these questions myself, standing at a crossroads that seemed to hold the weight of my past and the potential of my future.

Then there are few who thought they had mapped out their lives, whether it is the guy who wants to reverse age by spending millions of dollars every year or geniuses like Steve Jobs whose sole aim in life is to change the world but, halfway through that goal, leave planet Earth on an urgent mission.

For a long time, I thought I had my life mapped out. Like many, I stepped into adulthood with a sense of purpose, a drive to create something meaningful, and the hope that each choice would bring me closer to gratification. But life doesn't always (or never) unfold in a predictable way, and along the journey, I encountered challenges that revealed more about myself than I ever anticipated. I came face to face with fears I didn't know I had, insecurities I thought I had left behind, and the realization that, perhaps, I was just as lost as anyone else.

THE FEAR OF THE UNKNOWN – LESSONS IN COURAGE

Fear has a way of shaping our choices, sometimes quite drastically and often without us even realizing it. In the early stages of my life, I always made choices that felt safe. They were decisions that seemed to align with the expectations around me and paths that others had walked before. But at a certain point, I began to feel the hollow ache of complacency, of a life that looked fine on the surface but was missing something deeper. It became clear that I was being called to step out of my comfort zone, venture into the unknown, and confront the parts of myself that felt unfulfilled.

That choice to step into the unknown was terrifying. I stumbled, made many mistakes, and sometimes doubted whether I was on the right path. But through each experience, I learned that fear, when faced, has a way of becoming smaller. It no longer holds the same power over me, and with every step, I grow a little more resilient, a little surer of who I am becoming.

GROWTH THROUGH STRUGGLE – THE BRIDGE BETWEEN WHO I WAS AND WHO I AM BECOMING

We all carry a version of ourselves that feels familiar and comfortable. But if we are honest, there's always another version we are reaching for, a vision of who we could be if we had the courage to evolve. My journey has been a constant push and pull between these two selves. I have seen the person I am that was shaped by my past and the person I want to be, defined by growth and purpose.

It's never been an easy journey. In moments of struggle, it's tempting to retreat to return to the safety of the known. I have done it myself, choosing the path of least resistance and then feeling the persistent nudge to try again. Each setback has taught me something about resilience, the power of persistence, and the importance of pushing through, even when the way forward is unclear.

Through these experiences, I have come to see that growth does not come from ease; rather, it comes from stepping into discomfort, from challenging myself to break free of old patterns and create new ones. The bridge between who I was and who I am becoming is built on these choices, small moments of courage that add up to transformation.

THE POWER OF FORGIVENESS AND LOVE: UNLEASHING FREEDOM WITHIN

As I have grown, one lesson has stood out among the rest: the power of forgiveness and love. At certain points in my life, I carried resentment, anger, and regret like heavy stones. I blamed others, circumstances, and even myself for the way things unfolded. But as the years went on, I realized that these feelings were not serving me well. They were shackles binding me to the past and limiting my capacity to fully live in the present.

Forgiveness became a very important step, not just for others but for myself. It wasn't easy. Letting go of resentment felt like letting go of a part of me. But forgiveness isn't about really excusing what happened; it's about freeing yourself from the burden of carrying it. In that freedom, I found space for something deeper: love. This was not just love for others but a sense of love for life itself, a love for the journey, however messy and unpredictable it may be.

EMBRACING MORTALITY – THE URGENCY OF LIVING FULLY

At some point, the reality of mortality became a pressing thought. I began to understand that life isn't an endless resource. It's finite, fleeting, and precious. A powerful clarity came with this realization. It forced me to ask myself, "If I only have this one life, how am I going to live it?"

This unique understanding shifted my perspective. I stopped seeing time as something to constantly fill and started viewing it as something to really cherish. Each moment, each choice, became an opportunity to live more fully, love more deeply, and pursue what truly mattered to me and the people I care for. I wanted to live in a way that when the end finally came, I could look back without regret, knowing I had lived true to myself. When I die, I want a smile on my face, telling me that I lived life on the terms I intended.

THE INVITATION TO EXPLORE THE UNCHARTED

Life is a journey we're all navigating, each of us with our own unmarked map, our own questions, our own crossroads. I don't claim to have all the answers. I'm still learning, still growing, and still facing challenges that push me beyond my comfort zone. But what I do know is this: the journey is worth it. The discomfort, the struggles, the moments of doubt are all part of the path guiding us toward something greater.

This book is an invitation to step into the uncharted territory of your life, confront the fears, push through the doubts, and embrace the unknown. It's an invitation to live fully, forgive freely, love deeply, and be brave enough to seek the person you're meant to become.

As we begin this journey together, remember that you are not alone by any means. The world is dramatically changing beneath us, driven by greed, technology, and the desire for dominance. We are all navigating this complex, beautiful, messy thing called life. While the path may be uncertain, each choice, each moment, and each step forward brings us closer to the life we are meant to live. So, take a deep breath, gather your courage, and let's walk this path together into the uncharted.

ONE
THE IMPULSE WITHIN
NAVIGATING THE TENSION BETWEEN AUTHENTICITY AND EXPECTATION

Life has never been linear for me. From my earliest days, I realized that I didn't experience the world in the way others did. My impulsive nature, shaped by neurodivergence, often drove me in unexpected directions, sometimes leading to extraordinary outcomes and, at other times, creating challenges I struggled to overcome.

But the decisions I made were rarely calculated; they always came from a raw place of intuition, a deep-seated urge to act immediately based on what felt right. More often than not, my impulses helped me do the right thing, but at other times, they led me into conflict, especially with people whose behavior didn't align with my sense of fairness. When it came to matters of love, I struggled to tell people they were wrong or untrustworthy, preferring to avoid conflict, take the blame, and move on, which continued to add emotional debt.

Neurodivergence has brought with it a heightened sense of awareness of both the world and myself, but it has also brought emotional intensity. My emotions have never been quiet; they're loud, insistent, and often overpowering. I've never played by the rules of being "nice" for the sake of societal comfort. I wasn't built to mask my true feelings or sugarcoat my dissatisfaction when I see people behaving wrongly, particularly with matters of the heart.

I've often stood up and called out what I've perceived to be unjust, even when it came at the expense of my own peace, relationships, or success. This raw, unfiltered honesty became my guiding force, but it also turned impulsive decisions into bad ones, especially when driven by emotion rather than a calculated strategy.

However, a deeper conflict is at play that is not unique to me. Each of us, in our own way, battles between being true to ourselves and trying to fit into a world that values conformity. Neurodivergence only amplifies that battle. The brain processes things differently, emotions are felt with greater intensity, and the line between impulse and reflection blurs. Many people live with similar experiences, perhaps not from neurodivergence but from other struggles, mental health challenges, personal conflicts, or societal pressures that make life's path more turbulent for them than it might seem for others.

Despite my neurodivergent mind, which often pushes me to act in extremes, I've always focused on doing what I felt was right, not for the sake of money or material success but because it aligned with my values. That said, I've encountered situations where doing the right thing didn't bring the results I expected. In fact, focusing on the greater good often didn't bring financial gain; it brought emotional satisfaction and a sense of alignment with my true self, but not always the kind of success the world rewards.

This inner conflict between staying authentic and achieving conventional success is not exclusive to me. Steve Jobs, for instance, was notorious for his impulsive decisions and refusal to compromise his vision. His neurodivergent tendencies, often marked by obsessive focus and bursts of creative genius, enabled him to revolutionize the tech industry. However, the exact same behavior also alienated people and created conflict. He was driven by a vision so intense that it often came at the expense of relationships and personal well-being. Jobs didn't play by the rules of being "nice"; he played by the rules of truth, no matter the cost.

Similarly, Elon Musk, another figure often discussed in the context of neurodivergence, demonstrates how the brain's alternative wiring can lead to world-changing ideas. Musk, like Jobs, has spoken about his neurodivergence and how it shapes his relentless drive. Yet, for every innovation, he faces criticism—his impulsive tweets, erratic business decisions, and single-minded pursuit of goals sometimes leave damage in their wake.

Despite his fame and success, Musk often struggled with the same internal battle. Until recently, he stayed authentic, following his unique thought patterns while navigating the external consequences. However, his recent behavior is a more calculated strategy, the polar opposite of the version of himself that created much of his empire.

These figures, like many of us, struggle to balance their true selves with the expectations of the world. Their journeys remind us that success isn't always about money, fame, or accolades but about staying true to who you are, even if that means battling through conflict, dissatisfaction, or misunderstanding.

This has been my greatest challenge: learning how to honor my true self, navigating the impulsive decisions born from neurodivergence, and finding a balance between acting on principle and managing the fallout. I've found that doing the right thing—standing by my values—often yields results that align with my sense of purpose but not necessarily with financial success or public approval. Yet, I've never chased success in the traditional sense. For me, the real victory has always been about integrity, about living in alignment with who I am, even when the world doesn't understand or reward it.

The struggles I face are shared by many people out there—people who fight through the noise of societal expectations, people whose minds work differently, who feel emotions more deeply, and who question whether they're truly living authentically or just conforming to survive. It's the universal challenge of balancing between staying true to yourself and achieving success by the world's standards.

Fame and fortune often look glamorous from the outside, but many who achieve it face internal battles, just as we do. The conflict of living authentically while trying to meet the world's demands is a struggle we all share, regardless of the size of our platform. In the end, what truly matters isn't the material rewards—it's the peace that comes from knowing we stayed true to ourselves, neurodivergent or not, and pursued what we believed was right.

KEY THEMES:

1. **Impulsive Decision-Making and Its Dual Nature:** Impulse can both guide us toward doing what feels right and lead us astray, especially when driven by emotional reactions.
2. **Authenticity vs. Societal Expectations:** The conflict between staying authentic and conforming to societal norms or expectations for success.

3. **Neurodivergence:** The unique way neurodivergent individuals experience the world, which may include heightened emotions, sensitivity to injustices, and an amplified sense of impulse.
4. **Balancing Greater Good with Personal Sacrifice:** The challenge of standing up for what feels right, even when it doesn't yield tangible rewards.
5. **Fame and Success Aren't the End Goal:** Icons like Steve Jobs and Elon Musk remind us that fame and success come with personal struggles and that true fulfillment often lies elsewhere.

LESSONS AND REFLECTIONS:

1. **Balance Is Key:** Striking a balance between being true to yourself and navigating societal expectations is essential, though it will always be a challenge.
2. **Embrace Neurodivergence as Strength:** Instead of viewing impulsiveness or emotional intensity as flaws, embrace them as aspects of neurodivergence that can guide you to unique insights and decisions.
3. **Success Is Relative:** The conventional markers of success—money, fame, recognition—don't always align with personal fulfillment. The journey to finding your own definition of success is critical.
4. **Impulsivity:** Reflect on when impulse has helped you make the right decision and when it has steered you wrong. What patterns do you see in these moments? How can you harness impulse for good while tempering it when it might be destructive?
5. **Neurodivergence:** Acknowledge how your brain processes experiences differently from others. Instead of fighting those tendencies, consider how they can be a strength—whether in creative problem-solving or in your ability to see injustice and respond to it.
6. **Authenticity:** Ask yourself, "Am I living in alignment with my true self, or am I making decisions to fit societal expectations? How does this tension manifest in my daily life?"

ACTIONABLE STEPS:

1. **Mindful Decision-Making:** When faced with a significant decision, pause to reflect on the impulse behind it. Is it driven by emotion, principle, or external pressure? Take a moment to balance impulse with reflection.
2. **Channel Emotional Intensity Productively:** Whether through creative outlets (art, writing, etc.) or advocacy for causes you believe in, find a way to channel the intense emotions that come with neurodivergence into something constructive.
3. **Define Your Own Success:** Write down what success means to you. Does it involve financial freedom, emotional peace, strong relationships, or making an impact on others? Regularly revisit this definition and adjust it as needed, recognizing that it may not match societal standards.
4. **Celebrate Authenticity, Even When It's Hard:** Practice moments of unapologetic authenticity in your daily life—whether it's speaking your truth in a relationship, standing up for something at work, or expressing your emotions fully. Note the impact on your sense of peace and purpose.
5. **Look for Patterns in Decision-Making:** Reflect on past decisions, especially those driven by impulse. Journal about when these decisions have led to positive outcomes and when they've backfired. Use this to inform your future actions, aiming to temper impulsiveness when necessary.

CONCLUSION:

Life pulls us in different directions between what feels right and what's expected of us. It's not always easy to walk that line. But here's the thing: authenticity comes at a cost, and so does pretending to be someone you're not. Some days, you'll get it right. Other days, you'll second-guess everything. That's fine. Nobody has this all figured out. The goal isn't perfection; it's getting closer to your real self, one step at a time.

At the end of the day, what matters is that you're making choices you can live with, not ones designed to please people who won't be there when it counts.

TWO
QUANTUM SCIENCES AND KARMA
UNDERSTANDING THE FORCES THAT SHAPE OUR LIVES

From the moment we enter this world, we are shaped by forces beyond our understanding. These forces, whether physical, emotional, or spiritual, guide the course of our lives in ways that often feel inexplicable. Some point to science to explain the fabric of our reality, while others turn to spiritual beliefs like karma to make sense of the patterns and connections that seem to define our existence. But can these two seemingly opposite forces, Quantum Sciences, and Karma, work together to explain the choices we make, the struggles we face, and the outcomes we experience?

At its core, quantum science delves into the building blocks of our reality, uncovering the strange, often paradoxical behaviors of particles that make up everything around us. Quantum science reveals that, on a subatomic level, life is unpredictable. Probabilities, rather than certainties, determine the outcomes of events. This mirrors a truth we all experience; despite our best efforts to control outcomes, uncertainty always reigns supreme. We may act with intention, but the results of those actions can surprise us, often only becoming clear years or even decades later.

The choices we make today, however small or seemingly insignificant, plant seeds that will inevitably shape our future. Just as quantum particles influence one another, even from a distance, our actions ripple through time, affecting outcomes in ways we might not foresee. Whether in our relationships, careers, or personal growth, every decision we make plants a seed that will grow, often slowly, sometimes without our immediate awareness, but always with an impact that can manifest much later in life.

This is where karma, in its simplest form, enters the conversation. Karma suggests that the seeds we sow through our actions, both good and bad, eventually bring about corresponding results. It is a reminder that nothing we do exists in isolation. Our choices, actions, and even thoughts are part of a larger cosmic balance, and while the results might not be immediate, they are inevitable. The energy we put out into the world will return to us in one form or another, sometimes years or decades later.

Consider the case of Bernie Madoff, one of the most infamous examples of karma's slow but certain justice. For years, Madoff built one of the largest Ponzi schemes in history, promising returns to investors that were too good to be true. His manifested actions appeared to bring him success, power, and wealth, at least for a time.

However, the seeds of unchecked deception he planted eventually grew into a tangled web of lies that unraveled, devastating thousands of lives and leading to his ultimate downfall. Despite enjoying years of unparalleled success, karma, in the end, ensured that the results of his actions caught up with him. The choices Madoff made decades earlier came back to shape his future in ways he could never have predicted, ultimately leading to his imprisonment and disgrace.

There are countless stories of other figures who, despite achieving fame or success, could not escape the long-reaching effects of their choices. Whether through deceit, greed, or harmful behavior, their decisions eventually bore fruit but ultimately resulted in downfall or tragedy. These examples remind us that no matter how distant the consequences may seem, karma ensures that the seeds we plant today will bear fruit tomorrow.

In my life, this has been a constant source of reflection. The impulsive decisions I made, the stands I took, and the times I spoke my truth all planted seeds. Sometimes, the results of those actions were immediate, creating friction or leading to unexpected outcomes, but more often, the true impact only revealed itself much later.

I've seen how actions taken years ago, whether driven by integrity or emotion, shaped the course of my journey in ways I couldn't have predicted. Karma, like the unpredictable outcomes of quantum science, worked quietly in the background, slowly ensuring that the energy I put into the world would return to me, often when I least expected it.

The intersection of two critical mythical forces, quantum uncertainty and karmic balance, reveals a deeper truth about life's journey. While science explains the unpredictability of outcomes, karma assures us that nothing is without consequence. It suggests that there is a deeper web of cause and effect that links our actions to the experiences we attract. Even in moments when life feels chaotic or unfair, karma reassures us that the seeds we plant today—through our actions, words, and intentions—will inevitably grow into the reality we experience tomorrow.

The lessons here are not simple, nor are they universal. Like quantum particles, life is not deterministic. Our decisions, actions, and the energy we bring into the world don't guarantee a specific outcome. What we can take from quantum sciences and karma is the understanding that our choices matter. Even in the face of uncertainty, even when outcomes don't immediately reflect our intentions, our actions still leave a mark on the fabric of reality. In that sense, both science and spirituality are correct. The world is full of unknowns, but it is also a place where our actions, large and small, ripple outward, affecting the broader tapestry of our lives.

In the chapters ahead, I'll continue exploring this intersection of unpredictability and karmic consequence, reflecting on how my own neurodivergence plays a role in the way I navigate these forces. The heightened emotions, impulsivity, and deep sensitivity to injustice, shaped by my unique wiring, have influenced the paths I've taken, both in personal relationships and in the broader scope of life. In many ways, neurodivergence has been my version of quantum uncertainty—guiding me in directions I didn't always anticipate, yet helping me stay true to who I am, even in the face of societal expectations.

As we move forward, I invite you to reflect on your life: How have unseen forces, whether scientific or spiritual, shaped your choices? How do you navigate the unpredictability of life, and where do you find a balance between trusting your instincts and considering the long-term impact of your actions?

In the end, we are all part of this cosmic web, acting, reacting, and creating waves that ripple out into the unknown. It's up to each of us to decide how we engage with that uncertainty and what we make of the paths we're given.

KEY THEMES:

1. **Science and Spirituality:** Life is randomly mixed with both cold, hard logic and mystical beliefs. The analytical world of

quantum uncertainty reminds us that randomness is part of the game, and similarly, the spiritual world of karma suggests there's a kind of cosmic balance at play. It's like life is giving us a nudge to see things from both angles. When we adapt that perspective, the world starts to make a little more sense.

2. **Little Actions, Big Ripples:** Ever think about how the smallest things you do can have a huge impact? That offhand comment, the quick decision you barely thought about—it all sends ripples into the future. Most of us won't always be able to see how all of this plays out, but those ripples are there, quietly shaping the world in ways we can't even imagine.
3. **Embracing the Unknown:** Quantum physics tells us that uncertainty is just part of the deal and is built into the universe. And karma? It's like a gentle reminder that everything we do is connected. It's a weird but beautiful combo that pushes us to live with purpose, even when we have no clue what's coming next.
4. **Trusting the Process:** Here's the thing: the results of our actions don't always show up right away. Sometimes, it takes years or even decades—for the pieces to fall into place. That's exactly why patience and mindfulness are so important. Staying present and trusting the journey helps us handle the waiting game, knowing that every choice we make is part of something bigger.

LESSONS AND REFLECTIONS:

1. **Embrace Uncertainty:** Quantum sciences show us that not everything in life is predictable. Learn to find peace with the unknown, trusting that every action, though uncertain in outcome, has value.
2. **Plant Seeds for the Future:** Every action is a seed planted in the soil of your future. Even if the results aren't immediate, trust that what you sow today will shape your life tomorrow.
3. **Karma as Cosmic Balance:** Like karma, our actions create ripples that will return to us. The energy you put out, positive or negative, will inevitably shape the path ahead.

ACTIONABLE STEPS:

1. **Mindful Decision-Making**: When faced with uncertainty, pause to assess the energy behind your action. Do positive intentions drive them, or are they reactions to external pressure?
2. **Acceptance of Outcomes:** Learn to release attachment to specific outcomes. Whether you're making decisions for personal growth, relationships, or career, understand that outcomes aren't always within your control.
3. **Reflect on Karma's Impact:** Consider how your past actions, big and small, have shaped your present. Where can you see the results of past energy, and how can you direct future energy toward balance and fulfillment?

CONCLUSION:

Nothing in life happens in isolation. Every choice, every action, every moment connects to something bigger. Quantum science tells us reality is fluid, always shifting, and never fully predictable. Karma reminds us that what we put out comes back in ways we might not expect.

So, what do we do with that? We take responsibility not just for what happens to us, but for how we respond. We stop living as if everything is random and start seeing our choices as seeds…seeds that will eventually grow into something, whether we're ready for it or not.

Life won't always make sense, but that doesn't mean it's out of our hands.

THREE
LEADERSHIP, LEGACY, AND THE WEIGHT OF DECISIONS
A HARSH REALITY CHECK

Leadership is often glamorized, and the lure of power often draws us to pursue it. We are programmed to believe that leaders are visionaries, people who inspire, innovate, and bring positive change. The unspoken truth is that leadership is brutal and comes at a price. For every iconic leader we celebrate, there's a harsh reality we often ignore. The sacrifices, compromises, and heavy weight of decisions define not just leaders but everyone around them. Leadership isn't about being liked; it's about making tough choices that others are too afraid to make.

THE DOUBLE-EDGED SWORD OF LEGACY

Legacy is the mark we leave on the world. It's the sum of our choices, achievements, and failures. If you peel back the layers, you'll see that legacy is complicated. Every legacy has its shadows, and the weight of that reality falls squarely on the shoulders of the leader.

Think of controversial leaders like Steve Jobs and Elon Musk. They are celebrated for their bold vision and relentless drive. However, behind the scenes, their paths were marked by hard and often ruthless decisions.

Jobs, for example, was known for his uncompromising vision. He demanded perfection from everyone around him. That drive created some of the most iconic products in history, but it also left a trail of people who felt abandoned, dismissed, or even broken by his intense expectations.

Jobs's legacy is a testament to genius, but it's also a reminder that greatness often comes at a deep personal cost to the leader and to those who follow.

Elon Musk is another example of a leader who is both revered and criticized for his leadership style. His relentless pursuit of a future on Mars, his uncompromising standards, and his desire to challenge the status quo have made him a polarizing figure across the world. The massive wealth he has accumulated now gives him the power to single-handedly influence who can run a country.

Musk is a visionary, yes, but his methods can be brutal. He has been criticized for pushing his employees to their limits, for making audacious and risky decisions, and for sometimes discarding those who don't fit into his grand vision. His legacy is still in the making, but one thing is clear: Musk is not interested in being liked; he's interested in achieving the impossible.

THE BURDEN OF TOUGH DECISIONS

Leadership is often about making decisions that others choose to avoid. Choices aren't always black and white for people in positions of power. Sometimes, the right decision isn't the popular one, and often, it's the choice that leaves scars. History's most impactful leaders understood this. True leaders understand that authentic leadership requires stepping into challenging situations, making sacrifices, and bearing the consequences of those decisions even after others have moved on.

Abraham Lincoln faced this very challenge during the Civil War. He carried the unimaginable burden of a deeply divided nation, and every decision he made was a gamble with human lives, national unity, and his legacy. The Emancipation Proclamation, for instance, was a decision that changed the course of history, but it was not an easy one for him to make. It was met with backlash, resistance, and doubt. Lincoln chose it, knowing that it would mark him forever, that he would face harsh criticism and bear the emotional toll. His legacy as the Great Emancipator is celebrated today, but it came at a tremendous personal and political cost.

This is the reality of leadership. It's not about being celebrated or remembered as a hero. It's about making decisions that serve a greater purpose, even if it means sacrificing oneself along the way. Leaders like Lincoln, Jobs, and Musk reveal a harsh truth: to lead is to take on a weight that most people would crumble under, to embrace a legacy that is as much a burden as it is a mark of greatness.

EMPATHY AND THE UNCOMPROMISING PATH

For many, the path of an uncompromising leader may seem ruthless or disconnected from empathy. But true empathy in leadership isn't about coddling or avoiding conflict. It's about understanding the stakes and the impact of each choice and making decisions that serve a greater purpose, even if it means making unpopular moves.

Nelson Mandela is a powerful example of empathy in leadership. His path was anything but easy. His empathy wasn't rooted in weakness; it was a fierce, determined empathy that fought against an unjust system. He sacrificed his freedom, suffered 27 years in prison, and, upon his release, bravely chose reconciliation over revenge. Mandela's empathy was uncompromising, driven by a vision for a unified South Africa, not a desire to be seen as kind or forgiving.

Leadership with empathy means making hard choices with a full understanding of their impact. It's not about pleasing people; it's about making decisions that are aligned with one's values and vision, even when it's painful.

THE WEIGHT OF ANALYSIS – LEARNING FROM LEGACY

What can we learn from these greatest leaders of generations? Their lives offer a blueprint for the cost and complexity of real leadership. If we strip away the praise and criticism, we see that these leaders were people who made choices—often hard, sometimes unpopular—that shaped their legacies. They were willing to stand alone, bear the weight of their decisions, and face the harsh judgment of others.

For those of us striving to lead in any capacity, these stories are a reminder of what true leadership demands. It requires a commitment to unwavering values, a willingness to sacrifice, and the resilience to keep going when the path is lonely. It is about understanding that each decision we make is a brick in the legacy we leave behind.

Real leadership is not for the faint-hearted. In a world that celebrates success but often ignores the personal cost, the stories of uncompromising leaders serve as a great reminder. Real leadership is for those who are willing to stand by their decisions, face their own imperfections, and leave a legacy that's as complex and layered as they are.

ANALYSIS AND REFLECTION – THE ANATOMY OF DECISION-MAKING

So, what does this mean for those of us who aren't on the world stage or shaping nations or industries? It means that every choice we make matters. Every decision, whether big or small, creates a ripple effect that defines not just our lives but the lives of those around us.

As leaders, we must ask ourselves whether we are willing to shoulder the responsibility for the outcomes of our decisions. Are we prepared to endure criticism, make sacrifices, and bear the burden of our choices?

Great leaders like Lincoln, Mandela, Jobs, and Musk demonstrate that leadership isn't about avoiding mistakes or seeking approval. Instead, it's about being authentic to a vision, standing steadfast in the face of challenges, and accepting that not everyone will comprehend or concur with our decisions.

Leadership is an art, a balance of empathy and conviction and a blend of heart and willpower. It's how your legacy is built, step by step, brick by brick, through choices that often feel like sacrifices. In the end, it's the weight of these decisions, their impact, their depth, and their legacy that reveals the true character of a leader.

EMBRACING THE UNCOMPROMISING PATH

The world doesn't need more leaders who play it safe. It needs leaders who are willing to be bold, to be decisive, to be uncomfortable. It needs people who understand that leadership isn't about personal gain but about making decisions that ripple far beyond themselves.

To those who dare to lead, remember that the path is not easy. You will face criticism, isolation, and the weight of choices that very few will understand. But know that every step, every decision, every sacrifice is part of a larger legacy. It's a legacy not just of success but of resilience, courage, and the willingness to embrace both the beauty and brutality of true leadership.

In the end, leadership is about standing in the space where empathy meets strength and conviction meets compassion. It's about knowing that while the world may not always see or understand our choices, the inedible mark we leave will speak for itself. The legacy of a leader is not in the praise they receive but in the lasting impact they make. For those willing to walk this path, that impact is all that matters.

KEY THEMES:

1. **The Duality of Legacy:** A leader's legacy is often a blend of brilliance and, most times, built around personal cost and sacrifices. Success is accompanied by tough choices and sacrifices that shape not only the leader but everyone around them.
2. **Empathy in Decision-Making:** Effective leadership requires balancing empathy with the courage to make unpopular decisions for a greater purpose.
3. **Long-Term Responsibility:** Leadership is about creating a vision and accepting the weight of its long-term impact, even when outcomes are uncertain or controversial.
4. **The Human Cost of Vision:** Leaders like Steve Jobs and Elon Musk exemplify how an uncompromising pursuit of goals can inspire transformation yet come at a high personal and relational cost.

LESSONS AND REFLECTIONS:

1. **Every Decision Is a Seed:** Just like in karma, the choices we make today will shape our future. Leadership is about planting seeds that may take years to grow but will inevitably impact the world around us.
2. **The Weight of Leadership:** The decisions we make as leaders carry immense weight. Even when faced with uncertainty, leaders must understand that their choices will shape their legacy and the future of those they lead.
3. **Legacy Is Built Over Time:** Legacy isn't built in a single moment. It's constructed through the sum of countless decisions, actions, and moments of integrity. Whether you're leading a team, a family, or yourself, your legacy is the product of your consistent choices.

ACTIONABLE STEPS:

1. **Mindful Leadership:** When making decisions, consider the long-term impact. Ask yourself, "What legacy am I creating with this choice?" Take time to reflect on how each action contributes to the larger narrative of your life.
2. **Embrace Uncertainty in Leadership:** Leadership often requires making decisions in the face of unknown outcomes. Develop comfort with uncertainty, trusting that the seeds you plant will bear fruit over time.
3. **Consistent Integrity:** Make decisions that reflect your core values, even when those decisions are difficult or unpopular. Leadership is not about seeking approval; it's about staying true to yourself and your vision.

CONCLUSION:

Leadership is messy. It's not just about being admired. It's about making tough calls, taking risks, and sometimes standing alone. It's easy to talk about legacy as if it's something grand, but in reality, It's built in the small moments, the difficult conversations, and the decisions nobody else wants to make.

The truth is, you won't always get it right. Every leader, from history's greatest minds to today's most powerful figures, has faced failures. What separates them isn't perfection. It's the ability to own their choices, learn, and keep moving forward.

What kind of legacy are you leaving? Because whether you realize it or not, you're building one right now.

FOUR
NAVIGATING RELATIONSHIPS
THE COMPLEX DANCE OF CONNECTION AND SELF-IDENTITY

Relationships are the ultimate test of who we are. They hold up a mirror that equally reflects our strengths and beauty as well as our flaws, insecurities, and the hidden corners of our souls. At their core, relationships are more than shared moments or companionship. They're where we confront the essence of who we are and who we aspire to be. And yet, for something so fundamental to our existence, relationships remain the most complex, often turbulent aspect of our lives.

Each relationship is a dance—a delicate balance between two people's needs, dreams, and fears. Some partners move in harmony, while others struggle, stepping on each other's toes in an attempt to lead. As we move through life, we enter and exit relationships. Each one taught us something about ourselves, often in the most unexpected ways.

THE PULL OF FAMILIARITY AND THE FEAR OF VULNERABILITY

Why do we choose to let certain people into our lives? More often than not, we gravitate towards those who feel familiar and what we miss in our relationships. Perhaps they remind us of a past love, a close friend, or even a family member. We identify with the positive traits and discount the red flags. There's a comfort in the familiar, a sense of safety. But in the pursuit of that safety and familiarity, we sometimes find ourselves trapped, repeating old patterns and seeking validation rather than growth.

Vulnerability is terrifying, even though it's the foundation of real connection. To truly love someone is to expose parts of ourselves that we often keep hidden, even from ourselves. But vulnerability comes with the risk of rejection, misunderstanding, or heartbreak. So, instead of opening up, we hold back and maintain a guarded distance that limits the depth of our relationships.

Think about how many times we've chosen the safer path, the one that allows us to keep our defenses intact. We engage in surface-level conversations, avoid confrontation, and shy away from revealing our true emotions. Most importantly, we run away from probing into that red flag. In doing so, we miss out on the beauty of genuine connection, sacrificing depth for comfort.

LOVE, EXPECTATIONS, AND THE SHADOW OF SELF-DOUBT

Every relationship carries a set of expectations, some spoken, others silent. We look to our partners to fulfill roles—friend, confidant, lover, support system. But when those expectations go unmet, disappointment and frustration follow. Love is often sold to us as unconditional, yet we frequently attach conditions, believing our happiness depends on someone else's actions.

True love is as much about managing our expectations as it is about nurturing the connection. Self-doubt often sneaks in, whispering that we're not enough and we don't deserve the love we seek. So, we grandly project these insecurities onto our partners, putting the burden on them to fill voids that only we can address within ourselves. More often than not, in a rush to nurture a connection, we discount the insecurities of our partners, giving them a way to hide or create a façade that they can't break in the future as they grow behind it.

The truth is, no partner can complete us. They can support, challenge, and inspire us, but the journey to self-acceptance is one we must walk alone. Relationships can be powerful catalysts for growth if they are approached with self-awareness and the recognition that our worth isn't tied to someone else's opinion or affection.

THE FRAGILE DANCE BETWEEN FREEDOM AND COMMITMENT

Commitment and freedom seem at odds with each other, yet they are both essential for a fulfilling relationship. We want the security of knowing someone is by our side, and simultaneously, we crave the space to grow and explore as individuals. It's a balancing act, one that many struggle to maintain.

Some relationships become cages, stifling our dreams and individuality. In our desire to keep a connection intact for the very reason of identifying what we are missing, we often lose sight of who we are, bending and reshaping ourselves to meet another's expectations. This sacrifice might sustain the relationship temporarily, but in the long run, it breeds resentment and stifles true intimacy, as the façades are destined to break.

True commitment never demands the loss of self. It encourages and nurtures a partnership that fuels growth and celebrates individuality while promoting the bond. When two people support each other's evolution, they create a relationship that's both grounded and expansive, one that allows for both stability and freedom.

LETTING GO – THE UNSPOKEN ART OF LOVE

One of the hardest truths about relationships is that to love sometimes means to let go. We often cling to relationships that have outlived their purpose, holding on out of fear, habit, or a sense of obligation. We convince ourselves that staying is a sign of loyalty, a testament to love, when, in reality, it may be preventing both people from growing.

Letting go is not a sign of failure; it's a sign of respect. We owe respect to ourselves as much as to the other person. It's acknowledging that sometimes, the most loving thing we can do is allow ourselves and our partner the freedom to move forward. This act of letting go requires immense courage, but it opens up space for both people to find deeper, more fulfilling connections.

THE IMPERFECT REALITY OF LOVE

Real love is messy, imperfect, and sometimes horridly painful. It's not the fairy tale we imagined or are programmed to believe. It's a journey that tests us, pushes us, and reveals parts of ourselves we didn't know existed. Love brings with it both joy and sorrow, growth and challenge, comfort and discomfort. Through it all, it teaches us a powerful lesson: love is not something we find; it's something we create.

In every relationship, there's a choice—to show up, to be vulnerable, to accept the imperfections in both ourselves and our partner. It's a conscious decision to love, even when it's difficult, to forgive, even when it hurts, and to let go, even when it's heartbreaking.

In the end, relationships are not about perfection; they're about growth. They're not about finding someone to complete us but finding someone who complements us as we both continue to evolve. Relationships are a complex dance, one that requires balance, resilience, and the courage to step into the unknown.

KEY THEMES:

1. **The Balancing Act Between Freedom and Commitment:** Every relationship is a push and pull. You want to be your own person, but you also want something real with someone else. A solid relationship respects individuality while keeping a foundation of trust strong enough to hold both people together—even when things get messy.
2. **Connection Is Fragile, Even When It Feels Solid:** Relationships need constant tending, like a fire that dies if you stop feeding it. The problem? Familiarity makes it easy to stop paying attention. You assume things are fine—until one day, you realize you've ignored the growing distance for too long.
3. **Being Vulnerable Feels Risky, But It's the Only Way:** Let's be real: putting your real self out there is scary. What if they don't get it? What if they leave? But if you're always guarding yourself, what's the point? The strongest relationships aren't the ones where you're perfect all the time; they're the ones where you're real, flaws and all.
4. **Letting Go for Growth**: True love sometimes means letting go, as clinging to connections that no longer align can hinder both personal and relational evolution.

LESSONS AND REFLECTIONS:

This chapter invites you to reflect on a few key points that shape our relationships:

1. **Familiarity vs. Growth:** Recognize when you're choosing relationships or behaviors out of comfort rather than the desire to grow. Growth often requires stepping out of the familiar and embracing vulnerability.
2. **Self-Identity and Expectations:** Understand that while relationships can offer support, they cannot define your self-worth. Be mindful of the expectations you bring and recognize the importance of fulfilling your own needs and dreams.
3. **Freedom and Commitment:** Healthy relationships allow space for individuality. A fulfilling commitment is not about restriction but supporting each other's personal growth.
4. **Letting Go:** Sometimes, the most loving act is letting go. Holding onto relationships out of fear can limit both you and your partner. Letting go can create room for both to grow in new directions.

ACTIONABLE STEPS:

These insights can become powerful tools for building stronger, healthier relationships:

1. **Examine Your Patterns:** Reflect on whether you're choosing relationships based on comfort or true connection. Challenge yourself to be open and vulnerable, even if it feels uncomfortable.
2. **Assess Your Expectations:** Think about the expectations you bring into your relationships. Are they realistic, or are they rooted in your insecurities? Focus on building a connection based on mutual support rather than on the fulfillment of unmet needs.
3. **Foster Balance:** Work toward a balance between commitment and independence. Talk openly with your partner about your need for both security and space to grow as individuals.

4. **Practice Letting Go** When Necessary: If you find yourself holding onto a relationship that no longer aligns with who you are, ask yourself whether it's time to let go. Remember that letting go can be an act of love, allowing both you and your partner the freedom to pursue what truly fulfills you.

CONCLUSION:

No relationship is simple. People are complicated, feelings shift, and misunderstandings happen. The question isn't whether relationships will challenge you—it's how you'll handle it when they do.

Real connection takes work, honesty, and the willingness to show up, even when it's uncomfortable. It means acknowledging your own flaws, recognizing the patterns that keep repeating, and choosing to be better—not just for others, but for yourself.

If nothing else, remember this: love isn't about perfection. It's about showing up, staying present, and growing together, even when it's hard.

FIVE
THE INNER STRUGGLE
MANAGING IMPULSIVITY AND FINDING BALANCE

As we keep pushing forward, wrestling with the contradictions of our existence—some under our control, others completely out of our hands—we eventually slam into one of the hardest battles: the one within ourselves. And the toughest fight? Managing the pull of impulse. For those of us who feel emotions and desires like a wildfire, that struggle never really ends.

It's not just about resisting temptation or making the 'right' choices. It's about knowing when to trust your gut and when to pull the brakes. Some people move through life with an easy sense of restraint. For the rest of us, every decision feels like a tug-of-war between instinct and consequence. And if you've lived long enough, you know that one reckless moment, one unchecked impulse, can rewrite the entire story. But without taking risks, without stepping into the unknown, are we even really living?

This isn't about controlling every reaction—it's about knowing which ones are worth acting on. Some impulses lead to breakthroughs. Others burn everything to the ground. Learning to tell the difference? That's the real work.

In the previous chapters, we touched on how life is shaped by the seeds we plant through our decisions, influenced by our programming and the unpredictable forces of karma and fate. But what happens when our actions are driven by impulse rather than careful reflection? How do we find the balance between spontaneity and mindfulness?

Impulsivity, for me, has often been a double-edged sword. At times, it has led to decisions that felt right in the moment and choices born from deep conviction, authenticity, and an immediate sense of justice. More often than not, impulsivity has created challenges, leading to outcomes I hadn't anticipated or conflicts I could have completely avoided.

Impulsivity, fueled by emotions that hit hard and fast, often makes us move before we think. Sometimes, it works out. Other times, it blows up in our face. But every choice—reckless or careful—leaves a mark, whether it pushes us forward or forces us to learn the hard way.

But I am not alone in this struggle. Many people, especially those who are like me, often experience life through the lens of heightened emotions or neurodivergence and find themselves battling between acting on instinct and pausing to reflect. The world tells us to think before we act and to measure our steps carefully. Yet, how do we reconcile that with the spontaneous moments that sometimes define our greatest successes—or lead to our deepest regrets?

Managing impulsivity doesn't mean stifling it altogether. It means finding balance—knowing when to lean into your instincts and when to take a step back. In the previous chapters, we explored how every decision plants a seed that shapes our future. This applies as much to the impulsive actions we take in the heat of the moment as it does to the carefully thought-out choices we make after reflection. Every move we make, even the ones that feel reckless, contributes to our personal growth and the larger story of our lives.

Look at figures like Steve Jobs and Elon Musk, whose impulsive decisions often shaped their legacies in dramatic ways. Jobs was notorious for making gut-driven, sometimes controversial decisions that alienated people but led to some groundbreaking innovations. Musk, with his impulsive public statements and unpredictable business moves, often walks a fine line between genius and recklessness. Both men, though, found ways to channel their impulsivity into creating something larger than themselves, even when the path wasn't always smooth.

But while these leaders embraced their impulsiveness, they also understood the importance of learning from their mistakes. Jobs, for instance, evolved over time, becoming more reflective in his decision-making while still staying true to his creative instincts. Musk, though still erratic at times, has shown an ability to course-correct when his impulsive actions lead to unintended consequences. Both men demonstrate that balance is key—that is, knowing when to act on impulse and when to step back and reassess the situation.

For me, the challenge has always been learning to pause in those moments when impulsivity threatens to override reason. I've found that some of the most critical moments in my life came when I was able to recognize the urge to act and instead chose to reflect. Not every decision needs to be immediate. Sometimes, the most powerful moves are the ones we make after giving ourselves the space to breathe, think, and consider the broader implications of our actions.

In life's dance, impulsivity can be a beautiful force—it pushes us out of our comfort zones, encourages creativity, and drives us to take bold risks. But to truly master the dance, we must also learn when to hold back, find our center, and move with purpose rather than just reaction. This balance is the key to navigating both the internal and external forces that shape our lives.

FINDING BALANCE

Finding balance doesn't mean suppressing who we are or denying our natural impulses. It means understanding when to act with spontaneity and when to embrace stillness. It means accepting that both the leaps we take and the moments of hesitation are part of the same dance. Just as we discussed in the earlier chapters, life isn't about escaping the forces that shape us but about learning to live consciously within them.

As you move forward in your journey, I invite you to consider your impulses. When do they serve you, and when do they lead you astray? What can you learn from the moments when you acted on instinct, and how can you find more balance between action and reflection in the future?

Life keeps pushing you forward. Sometimes you plan it, sometimes you just react. But either way, you're shaping where you end up. Trying to get your head and your heart on the same page, that's the trick.

KEY THEMES:

1. **Impulsivity:** Your Best and Worst Friend: Acting on impulse can feel like magic. You trust your gut and make a bold move. Sometimes, it works out brilliantly. Other times? Not so much.

The trick isn't to suppress your instincts but to know when to slow down and think before you jump.

2. **When to Trust Instinct vs. When to Hit Pause:** Some decisions are best made in the moment. Others? Not so much. Learning when to follow an impulse and when to step back is one of those hard-earned life lessons that only experience can teach you.
3. **Mistakes Suck, But They're the Best Teachers:** Nobody likes screwing up, but let's be real—half the things we actually learn come from falling on our faces. The only real mistake is not paying attention to what went wrong and trying to avoid it next time.
4. **Living with an Intense Mind:** If your brain runs at 100 mph all the time, slowing down isn't always easy. But the goal isn't to mute that intensity—it's to direct it. People with heightened emotions, especially neurodivergent folks, often struggle with balance, but that same intensity can fuel creativity and drive.

LESSONS AND REFLECTIONS:

1. **Impulsivity as a Double-Edged Sword:** Impulsiveness can lead to great breakthroughs or unanticipated challenges. Learning when to trust your instincts and when to pause for reflection is crucial.
2. **Balance Between Spontaneity and Mindfulness:** Finding balance doesn't mean suppressing impulsiveness but knowing when it serves you and when it hinders you.
3. **Personal Growth Through Mistakes:** Even when impulsive decisions lead to mistakes, they can be valuable learning experiences that contribute to long-term growth.

ACTIONABLE STEPS:

1. **Practice Mindful Decision-Making:** The next time you feel the urge to act on impulse, take a moment to pause. Ask yourself, "Is this a decision I need to make now? Will this choice contribute to my long-term goals?"

2. **Channel Impulsivity Productively:** Rather than stifling impulsive tendencies, find outlets where they can serve you. In creativity, leadership, or relationships, find areas where spontaneity can be an asset rather than a liability.
3. **Reflection as a Habit:** Regularly reflect on past decisions—especially those made impulsively. What worked? What didn't? How can you apply these lessons moving forward to create a better balance between impulsivity and thoughtful action?

CONCLUSION:

Impulse isn't the enemy—it's how you use it that matters. Some of the best things in life come from taking a chance, making a bold move, trusting your gut. But just as easily, impulse can pull you into situations that cost more than they're worth.

The key is learning to recognize when to trust yourself and when to hit pause. That balance? It takes time, experience, and plenty of mistakes.

You won't always get it right, but as long as you're learning from each misstep, you're moving in the right direction. Control isn't about shutting down who you are—it's about making sure you're the one steering the wheel.

SIX
THE INNER STRUGGLE
EMBRACING IMPERFECTIONS AND FINDING BALANCE

We all carry a storm within us, a mix of ambition, insecurity, anger, love, and the relentless drive to become something more. We're constantly at odds with ourselves, grappling with the push and pull of who we are versus who we want to be. This struggle isn't something we can simply ignore; it's woven into our very existence. The question isn't whether we have this inner conflict—it's whether we can face it, harness it, and let it shape us into something stronger.

In the quietest moments, when the world isn't looking, we confront parts of ourselves that are less than perfect. Our impulses, doubts, and anger rise to the surface, demanding attention. The truth is, there's an instinct within us that often works against our better judgment. We act impulsively, sometimes out of pride, sometimes out of fear, and sometimes because we're tired of holding back. More often than not, these impulses leave us questioning our choices and wondering if we're truly doing life right.

THE COST OF AUTHENTICITY IN A WORLD THAT DEMANDS NICENESS

Authenticity comes at a price. In a world that celebrates politeness and rewards those who play nice, there's a risk in showing up as your raw, unfiltered self. We're taught to present a version of ourselves that fits neatly into society's expectations. But when we choose authenticity over approval, we shake the ground beneath us, inviting judgment, misunderstanding, and often isolation.

Steve Jobs was infamous for his uncompromising authenticity. He didn't soften his words to make people comfortable. He demanded excellence with a ferocity that often bordered on abrasive. His approach alienated people, and he was widely criticized for his ruthless leadership style. Yet, his unyielding authenticity drove him to create some of the world's most iconic products. His legacy illustrates the cost of choosing truth over niceness; it shows us that authenticity, while often isolating, can be the catalyst for greatness.

In contrast, consider someone like Oprah Winfrey. Oprah's authenticity has always been laced with empathy and an understanding of people's struggles. She has built her empire not by pushing people away but by inviting them in and making them feel seen and heard. Oprah's authenticity is powerful, yet she balances it with kindness, showing us a version of truth that connects rather than divides. Both leaders have been authentic, yet their approaches show that there are different paths to wielding that authenticity.

EMBRACING IMPERFECTION – THE POWER IN OWNING OUR FLAWS

Perfection is an illusion. The more we strive for it, the more disconnected we become from our true selves. We live in a world that constantly tells us to improve, to be better, and to aim for an unattainable ideal. But what if the real strength lies not in erasing our flaws but in embracing them? What if the power lies in acknowledging that we are all works in progress, beautifully flawed and endlessly evolving?

Dwayne "The Rock" Johnson has built an entire brand on embracing his imperfections and using them to fuel his growth. He openly talks about his battles with depression, his failures in sports, and his struggles to find his place in the world. Instead of hiding his flaws, he shares them, making them part of his narrative. By doing so, he's shown that strength isn't about appearing perfect; it's about being real and allowing others to see that journey of growth.

In contrast, someone like Martha Stewart, especially during her peak years, focused heavily on perfection. She created a brand that represented the ideal lifestyle, one free of visible flaws or weaknesses. Yet, when her personal life unraveled in the public eye, the contrast between her image and reality became painfully clear. Her journey reveals the risk of pursuing perfection too intensely—it can create a public persona that feels unattainable and even inauthentic. Whereas The Rock's approach draws people closer, Stewart's brand often makes people feel inadequate.

IMPULSE AND RESTRAINT – THE ETERNAL TUG-OF-WAR

Every one of us is locked in a battle between impulse and restraint. A part of us craves immediate satisfaction; it wants to act now and think later. Then there's the part that knows better, the part that urges caution, patience, and wisdom. This inner tug-of-war shapes our lives, often leading us down paths we didn't plan to take.

Consider the contrasting approaches of Elon Musk and Warren Buffett. Musk is a poster child for acting on impulse. His Twitter activity, impulsive statements, and rapid decision-making have led to some of the biggest breakthroughs and controversies of our time. Musk's impulses fuel his vision, but they also come with volatility, frequently landing him in hot water. His approach shows us that impulse can drive innovation, but it can also create chaos.

On the other hand, Warren Buffett epitomizes restraint. Known for his patient, long-term investment strategy, Buffett is a master of waiting for the right moment rather than jumping on every opportunity. He famously avoided the tech boom in its early stages, choosing instead to invest in industries he understood well. Buffett's approach demonstrates the power of patience and the value of avoiding impulsive decisions. Whereas Musk's impulses have led to rapid growth and innovation, Buffett's restraint has yielded steady, sustainable success.

FINDING BALANCE – THE ART OF SELF-ACCEPTANCE AMID CHAOS

Life is a balancing act, a delicate dance between holding on and letting go, between pushing forward and standing still. In a world that demands action, productivity, and progress, the idea of balance often feels elusive. But balance doesn't mean a life free of chaos; it means finding calm within that chaos and accepting that some parts of us will always be at odds with each other.

Eckhart Tolle, the spiritual teacher and author, is an example of someone who embraces balance and stillness amid chaos. He advocates for mindfulness, existing fully in the present moment, and letting go of the need to control every aspect of life. His teachings remind us that balance doesn't come from controlling the external world but from finding peace within.

Tolle's approach is a stark contrast to figures like Gary Vaynerchuk, who promotes relentless hustle and constant activity. Vaynerchuk's philosophy is one of nonstop momentum, pushing boundaries, and embracing the chaos of ambition.

Both approaches offer valuable lessons. Tolle's calm presence reminds us of the need for inner peace, while Vaynerchuk's energy exemplifies the thrill and momentum that come from pursuing our passions. Balance, it seems, is not a one-size-fits-all solution. It's about finding the rhythm that allows us to coexist with our impulses, doubts, and ambitions without losing ourselves in the process.

KEY THEMES:

1. **Being Real in a World That Expects Perfection**: It's hard to be yourself when everything around you pushes for a polished, perfect version of you. But the truth? Trying to fit in all the time drains the life out of you. Choosing authenticity isn't easy—it often comes with pushback, but it's the only way to really live.
2. **Flaws Make You Who You Are:** We all want to be better, but the idea that you have to "fix" everything about yourself is a trap. Mistakes, setbacks, and imperfections aren't just unavoidable—they're where the real learning happens.
3. **Impulse vs. Restraint—The Battle Never Ends:** Acting on instinct feels right in the moment, but sometimes, taking a step back makes all the difference. The challenge? Knowing when to go with your gut and when to take a breath before making a move.
4. **Turning Struggles into Strength:** People admire confidence, but they OFTEN connect with vulnerability. Look at someone like The Rock—he owns his struggles, and that's part of what makes him inspiring. Growth isn't about

pretending you've got it all figured out; it's about being open to the journey.

LESSONS AND REFLECTIONS:

The journeys of these leaders offer insights into our own inner struggles:

1. **Authenticity vs. Niceness**: Recognize that authenticity comes in many forms. For some, it's raw and unfiltered, while for others, it's softened with empathy. Choose the form that resonates with your truth, but remember that either path requires courage.
2. **Embracing Imperfections**: Look at your flaws as part of your narrative, as Dwayne Johnson does. Use them as fuel for growth instead of obstacles to overcome. Embrace the lessons that only imperfection can teach.
3. **Impulse vs. Restraint**: Both impulse and restraint have their place. The stories of Musk and Buffett remind us that while impulsiveness can drive innovation, restraint builds stability. Find a balance that serves your goals without compromising your values.
4. **Seeking Balance in Chaos**: Understand that balance doesn't always mean peace; sometimes, it means harnessing energy and chaos, as Vaynerchuk does. Other times, it means surrendering to the present moment, as Tolle teaches. Find your version of balance in this tug-of-war.

ACTIONABLE STEPS:

To integrate these insights into your life, follow these steps:

1. **Choose Your Authenticity**: Reflect on how you want to show up in the world. Whether you lean toward Jobs's blunt honesty or Oprah's empathetic connection, commit to a form of authenticity that aligns with who you are.
2. **Accept and Use Your Imperfections**: Like The Rock, share your imperfections rather than hide them. View them as stepping stones on your journey and use them to connect with others on a more genuine level.

3. **Balance Impulse and Restraint**: Ask yourself, "Is this decision driven by an impulse or a long-term vision?" Cultivate the awareness to know when it's time to act swiftly, like Musk, and when it's better to wait, like Buffett.
4. **Define Your Balance**: Reflect on whether you find balance in stillness (like Tolle) or action (like Vaynerchuk). Embrace the approach that feels most natural to you and recognize that balance is unique to each person.

CONCLUSION:

The idea that you have to fix yourself before you can be happy? It's a myth. You don't need to be perfect to be worthy, to be loved, or to find success. You just need to be real.

Flaws don't make you less. They make us human. And the second you start embracing them instead of hiding from them, life shifts.

So, stop waiting for the moment you "finally get it all together." Start now. Messy, imperfect, in progress. That's where the real transformation happens.

SEVEN
LOVE, LOSS, AND THE JOURNEY TO FINDING CONNECTION
IN THE SECOND HALF OF LIFE

Love is one of the most complex emotions, yet it is also the simplest. It defies logic, transcends time, and carries us to heights and depths we cannot anticipate. From our first cries at birth to the final breath we take, love, in all its forms—familial, romantic, and spiritual—shapes the essence of our being. As we move into the second half of life, love reveals its layers infused with loss, lessons, and an undeniable yearning for meaning. But then, with this revelation comes a reckoning: how do we navigate love's infinite complexities while staying true to ourselves and not getting sucked into the Maya? (A clouding of vision according to Hindu philosophy–we'll get more into this later.)

This stage of life forces us to confront not only the love we have received but also the love we failed to nurture. It asks us to evaluate the weight of our choices, the gaps we left unbridged, and the karmic imprints of our relationships. Love, in this phase, is no longer about passion alone; it is about purpose, resilience, and learning to balance the many dimensions of connection that make life whole.

THE SACRED BOND OF A MOTHER'S LOVE

My mother's love was and still is the foundation of everything good in my life and the cornerstone of my existence. She is truly my anchor, just as she is to all my siblings and their halves, a beacon of unconditional love that has never wavered, even in the most turbulent times.

Her love wasn't just expressed through grand gestures but in the small, everyday acts that spoke volumes. A simple question, "Did you eat?" could dissolve the weight of a thousand worries. It wasn't just a concern but a care distilled into its purest form. Her love was an unyielding presence that kept us grounded, even as life threw its fiercest storms our way.

Through her, I saw what it means to love unconditionally. Her good karma accumulated in ways that weren't always visible but were undeniably our protection. It was her quiet resilience, her ability to sacrifice without complaint, that became the shield for our family. When we faced challenges that should have broken us, her unwavering faith and love kept us intact. Even now, when she's not physically near, the thought of her can evoke emotion so raw it feels like a physical ache, reminding me of how deeply her love shaped me.

As a parent, I've tried to replicate that love for my own children. But life, as it often does, complicates the purest of intentions. The reality of two homes, a curse of modern relationships, created a painful distance that feels both unnatural and unavoidable. Sometimes, they are just a mile away, yet I cannot see them. That absence creates a void no amount of logic can fill. It hardens you and forces you to rationalize emotions you were never meant to suppress.

This duality of being the recipient of the greatest love while grappling with the gaping hole of not fully replicating it for my own children is a wound I carry. But wounds teach. They remind us of what matters most, of the love we must strive to give even when circumstances conspire to make it difficult.

WHY RELATIONSHIPS FALTER: THE CRACKS BENEATH THE SURFACE

The fragility of relationships often lies in what we overlook rather than what we confront. Love begins with a spark, a whirlwind of passion and idealism, but over time, the glow fades. When the novelty dissipates, what remains is often ignored: the hard work of understanding, forgiveness, and growth.

Many relationships fail because they are built on illusions. We fall in love with the idea of someone, not the reality. We chase perfection we can't describe or define, blinded by the glamor of the new, only to abandon ship when the flaws emerge. Instead of digging deeper, we look outward, seeking validation, excitement, or escape. In the process, we neglect the soil that could have nurtured something profound.

- **Parents and Children:** The bond between parents and children is, perhaps, unshakable, yet it is often taken for granted. Parents give endlessly, often losing themselves in the process, while children grow, drift, and sometimes fail to see the sacrifices made for them. Resentments fester in the gaps of unspoken expectations, turning love into obligation.
- **Siblings:** These relationships, rooted in shared history, often falter due to unresolved rivalries or diverging paths. The connection that should be a source of strength becomes a casualty of misunderstanding or neglect.
- **Couples:** Romantic relationships, the most fragile of all, are often doomed by superficial expectations. When the initial thrill fades, couples either grow together or drift apart. Often, they drift due to the allure of Maya, the illusion of something better, newer, or easier.

What's missing is the willingness to stay, to work, to see the flaws not as deal-breakers but as opportunities for growth. Love is not sustained by grand gestures or fleeting passion; it thrives in the quiet, consistent effort to truly know and be known by another.

THE ROLE OF MAYA AND KARMIC LESSONS IN LOVE

In Hindu philosophy, Maya is the illusion that clouds our vision, binding us to superficial desires and distractions. In love, Maya often manifests as infatuation or the pursuit of perfection. It blinds us to what is real, making us chase the shiny and new while ignoring the depth and substance that truly sustain relationships.

Yet, karma has a way of cutting through the fog. My mother's love, grounded and pure, taught me to see beyond illusions. But I have also been ensnared by Maya, making choices that felt right in the moment but lacked the foundation to endure. These missteps, while painful, were necessary. They taught me to value clarity over passion, substance over style, and purpose over convenience.

Karma tells us that every action we take has consequences, whether in this life or another. When it comes to love, karma can be both a blessing and a curse. Each relationship we enter leaves an imprint, a karmic residue that stays with us long after the relationship has faded. We carry the weight of our past loves, unfinished lessons, and unresolved conflicts. The choices we made in our youth, driven by impulse or passion, echo back to us, asking us to reflect, reconcile, and learn.

Think of figures like Johnny Cash, whose love for June Carter was both transformative and destructive. Their relationship had an undeniable magnetism, a karmic bond that defied logic, yet it came with heavy consequences. Cash's life was marked by addiction, turmoil, and loss, but through his connection with June, he found a glimpse of redemption. Their love was raw and flawed, an example of karmic forces at play, a love that required suffering and transformation to reach understanding.

In the second half of life, we begin to recognize these patterns. We see that love isn't just about finding someone who makes us happy; it's about understanding the karmic lessons we're here to learn. Every heartbreak, every disappointment, every cherished memory is a part of our soul's journey, pushing us to confront our deepest fears and our greatest aspirations. Love, then, becomes a crucible, a place where we are tested, where we break, and where—if we're lucky—we finally understand what it means to love unconditionally.

QUANTUM ENTANGLEMENT – THE MYSTERY OF CONNECTION

Quantum theory suggests that once two particles have interacted, they remain connected, no matter the distance between them. This theory, known as quantum entanglement, reflects a truth we often feel but cannot explain in words: we are connected in ways that transcend time and space. The people we love, the souls we touch, remain a part of us, even if they're no longer physically present.

This entanglement explains why we still feel the presence of loved ones who have passed, why memories of old relationships linger, and why certain connections feel destined. Think of Princess Diana, a woman who continues to impact the lives of millions. Her legacy, spirit, and compassion remain entangled with the world, affecting change long after her tragic death. Her life and death remind us that love is an energy that doesn't dissipate. Instead, it transforms, crossing dimensions and touching lives in ways we may never fully understand.

In the second half of life, we become more aware of this quantum entanglement. We sense that our relationships are not merely interactions but sacred connections that alter the fabric of who we are. Each person we love, each soul we encounter, leaves an indelible mark on our spirit. We begin to understand that love, like energy, cannot be destroyed; it only changes form, living on in memories, actions, and, sometimes, the haunting silence of our own hearts.

AFTERLIFE AND THE ULTIMATE REUNION

As we grow older, the question of what happens after death becomes more than just a philosophical inquiry. It becomes deeply personal. We wonder if the people we've lost, the loves we never let go, will be there waiting for us on the other side. We question if our connections in this life continue beyond the veil of mortality or if they fade into nothingness.

Religious and spiritual traditions offer various beliefs. Some speak of heaven, others of reincarnation, and still others of a universal consciousness where all souls are united. But perhaps the truth is beyond our comprehension. Perhaps, like in quantum physics, we exist in multiple states simultaneously, both here and there, both separate and connected.

The second half of life invites us to ponder these mysteries. When we lose someone we love, it often feels like a part of us has been ripped away. But with time, we begin to sense that they're still with us, guiding us, loving us from afar. This isn't mere sentimentality; it's a recognition of the soul's unbreakable connection to those it has loved. We realize that death may end a life, but it doesn't end a relationship. The love we share transcends this physical realm, living on in ways we may never fully understand.

LIVING WITH PURPOSE – THE CHOICE TO LOVE FEARLESSLY

In the face of love, loss, and the unknown, the greatest act of courage is to love fearlessly. By the time we reach the second half of life, we've seen how fragile love can be. We know that every connection comes with the risk of loss, and yet, to close ourselves off from love is to deny the very essence of life. We've witnessed too much to be naïve, but we've also learned enough to know that love is worth the pain, worth the uncertainty.

Consider Frida Kahlo and her tumultuous relationship with Diego Rivera. Their love was marked by passion, betrayal, separation, and reconciliation. Despite the pain, Frida continued to love with an open heart, channeling her experiences into her art. She chose to embrace the full spectrum of love, to live deeply, even if it meant suffering. Her life teaches us that love, in its truest form, is not about security or comfort; it's about diving into the unknown and accepting both the joy and the sorrow.

The second half of life invites us to make this same choice—to love with all we have, knowing that it may not last, that it may break us, but also knowing that it is the only thing that makes life truly meaningful. Love is the ultimate act of bravery, a defiance against the transient nature of existence, a declaration that, despite everything, we will continue to connect, open our hearts, and live.

THE IMPORTANCE OF 360° LOVE

A fulfilled life demands love that is multi-dimensional. The love of a parent grounds us, the love of children mirrors our strengths and flaws, and the love of a partner provides companionship and purpose. Neglecting any dimension creates an imbalance that leaves us unmoored.

But balance requires effort. It means showing up fully for the people who matter, even when it's inconvenient or uncomfortable. It means leaving work at work, setting aside ego, and prioritizing connection over conflict. It means choosing depth over surface, commitment over novelty, and substance over illusion.

PRACTICAL STEPS FOR BUILDING GROUNDED RELATIONSHIPS

1. **Communicate Beyond Words:** Ask questions that go deeper than the surface. With your parents, children, or partner, explore their fears, dreams, and regrets.
2. **Compartmentalize Pain:** Learn to leave work stress or relationship wounds where they belong. Protect your loved ones from becoming collateral damage.

3. **Invest in Substance:** Focus on shared values, trust, and emotional depth in relationships rather than surface-level compatibility.
4. **Nurture Every Dimension:** Give equal attention to parental bonds, sibling connections, and romantic partnerships. A fulfilled life requires balance.
5. **Practice Gratitude:** Reflect daily on the love you have received and given. Gratitude keeps you grounded and open to deeper connections.

KEY THEMES:

1. **Love Evolves, But It Never Gets Easier:** When you're younger, love is passion, excitement, and figuring out what you want. Later in life, it becomes about depth—learning how to hold onto what matters and let go of what doesn't.
2. **The Past Always Shows Up:** Whether you believe in karma or not, our past actions shape the way we love today. We repeat patterns, chase illusions (Maya), and sometimes don't realize we're caught in cycles until we stop and take a hard look at ourselves.
3. **Some Connections Never Fade:** You ever notice how some people stay with you long after they're gone? That's because real love—real connection—transcends time and space. The people who shape us never really leave us.
4. **Loving Without Fear, Even When You Know Loss is Inevitable:** Loss is part of love. You either let that reality keep you from opening up, or you embrace love anyway. The most meaningful relationships aren't the ones that last forever— they're the ones that change you.

LESSONS AND REFLECTIONS:

1. **Love as a Journey:** Love evolves and demands resilience, understanding, and a willingness to grow.
2. **Seeing Through Illusions:** Recognize the pull of Maya and seek connections that align with your true values.

3. **Multi-Dimensional Fulfillment:** True happiness comes from nurturing love in all its forms—familial, romantic, and spiritual.
4. **Karmic Lessons in Love:** Understand that each relationship, each heartbreak, and each joy is part of your soul's journey, a lesson in growth and understanding.
5. **Quantum Connection:** Recognize that love creates bonds that transcend physical distance and time. The people we connect with leave an eternal imprint on our lives that echoes long after they're gone.
6. **The Courage to Love:** Choose to love fearlessly, even knowing the risks. Love isn't about avoiding pain; it's about embracing life fully, with all its joy and sorrow.

ACTIONABLE STEPS:

These steps can help you embrace love and connection with greater depth and awareness:

1. **Reflect on Your Karmic Patterns:** Look at the patterns in your relationships. Are there lessons that keep repeating? Take time to understand what each relationship is teaching you about yourself.
2. **Honor Quantum Connections:** Make peace with the relationships that have left a mark on your heart. Send a silent thought of gratitude to those who've shaped your life, even if they're no longer present.
3. **Embrace Love Despite Loss:** Open your heart to love without fear. Let the stories of figures like Frida Kahlo remind you that love's value lies in its intensity and authenticity, not in its permanence.
4. **Contemplate the Afterlife:** Spend time in quiet reflection, pondering what you believe about life beyond this one. Allow this reflection to deepen your appreciation for the relationships and moments you experience now.

CONCLUSION:

Love is the thread that ties us to ourselves, each other, and the universe. It is both the most fragile and the most enduring force in our lives. My mother's love was my anchor, my children's love is my mirror, and the love I seek in a partner is the horizon toward which I walk.

Love is not perfect, and it never will be. But it is worth every risk, every sacrifice, every tear. To love is to live fully, to embrace the messy, beautiful truth of being human.

EIGHT
PARENTING IN THE PRESENT
NAVIGATING PARENTHOOD WITH MINDFULNESS AND INTENTION

Parenthood is often viewed as a duty we carry as part of our journey. But if we look deeper, we'll see that parenting is an act of co-creation, a role that shapes not only our children but also ourselves. True parenting is an evolving, raw, and intimate experience. When done with intention, it brings us face to face with our limitations, fears, and hopes. Parenting forces us to see life not just through our own eyes but through the vulnerable, impressionable lens of those we guide. It's a journey that demands us to be present and mindful and to approach each moment with intention.

In an ever-connected world that constantly distracts us from work with the destructive distraction of endless social media scrolling and confuses us with the relentless pursuit of success, being a present parent is a revolutionary act in itself. In the grand tapestry of life, the moments we spend guiding, nurturing, and loving our children become the threads that bind generations. Yet, the pace with which we are losing that connection is alarming, and what's coming for future generations is scary. The role of a parent isn't merely about raising a child but about influencing a soul, shaping a legacy, and planting seeds that will bear karmic fruits long after we exit this realm.

THE KARMIC INFLUENCE OF FATHERHOOD

Karma tells us that our actions, words, and intentions ripple outward, affecting not only our lives but also those who come after us. In fatherhood, this karmic influence is profound. Every choice we make, every value we instill, and every mistake we rectify or ignore creates a foundation that will impact generations. Our children inherit not just our physical traits but our karmic imprints, strengths, fears, aspirations, and, sometimes, our unhealed wounds.

Nelson Mandela, despite his absence due to lifelong imprisonment, left a legacy of resilience, forgiveness, and strength for his children and the world. His influence transcended his physical presence, leaving a karmic mark that shaped his family's identity and principles. Mandela demonstrated that fatherhood is not solely about being physically present. It's about being a guiding force, a beacon of values that stands the test of time. The karmic impact of our parenting reverberates through the lives of our children, influencing their choices and shaping their futures.

As parents, we have the opportunity and responsibility to break cycles of pain and address our own limitations so that we don't pass them on. Parenting is a chance to reflect on the imprints we're leaving to ask ourselves whether we're imparting values that uplift or burdens that weigh down. It's a role that requires us to look inward to confront our shadows and make peace with the parts of ourselves we don't want to pass down.

QUANTUM PARENTING – THE POWER OF PRESENCE

Quantum theory says that mere observation can influence the behavior of particles. The concept of presence in parenting takes on a similar role. Being truly present with our children, listening without distraction, and engaging with intention can shape their sense of self-worth, confidence, and identity in profound ways. In a world that's increasingly disconnected, this kind of presence has become rare, yet it's one of the most powerful gifts a parent can offer.

Barack Obama, despite the demands of his presidency, always made a point of being present for his daughters. He understood that parenting isn't about grand gestures but about quiet, consistent acts of love and attention. This intentional presence builds trust, creates security, and forms a foundation upon which children can grow. Our children don't need us to be perfect; they need us to be there, see them, witness their growth, and affirm their worth.

As parents, our presence or absence leaves an indelible mark. It's not the occasional moments of intensity that shape our children but the quiet, steady presence that makes them feel seen and valued. Each interaction, each shared moment, each time we put down our phone and truly engage is an investment in their future, an act of quantum parenting that impacts their self-perception and their ability to connect with others.

THE EXISTENTIAL WEIGHT OF FATHERHOOD

There's a profound existential weight to parenthood, a realization that we are shaping lives that will continue beyond our own. The best gift we can give our kids is not a bank account but preparing them to face the world just like every animal does to their offspring.

The world is ever-changing. What we see today will not exist a decade from now, and giving our children the personality, strength, and courage to inherit a world we may never see is a critical part of parenting. This understanding can be both daunting and liberating. We are reminded that our time here is finite and that the legacy we leave is woven through the lives of those we touch.

Philosophers and mystics alike have contemplated the role of parenthood in shaping the human soul. Parenting, they suggest, is not just an earthly duty but a spiritual path. It's an opportunity to refine ourselves, teach by example, and impart the wisdom we've gathered. The love we pour into our children becomes a form of immortality, a part of us that continues even when we are gone. Parenthood, then, becomes an act of transcending our ego, of recognizing that life is bigger than ourselves, that our children carry forward our lessons, our dreams, and, ultimately, our legacy.

MINDFUL PARENTING – CHOOSING THE PATH OF INTENTION

In this second half of life, parenting requires us to be intentional in a way that youth may have blinded us to. With each passing year, we become more aware of how fleeting time is. We understand that parenting isn't about controlling or molding our children. It is about guiding them while giving them the space to become who they're meant to be. It's about stepping back when necessary and trusting that the values we've imparted will serve them as they navigate the complexities of their lives.

Parenting with intention means choosing to be fully present, to listen, and to respond with empathy. It means recognizing that every one of our words, actions, and responses has an impact. It's a commitment to raise our children not just to survive in the world but to thrive, find purpose, and contribute meaningfully.

In the end, mindful parenting is about letting go of our desire for control. It's about understanding that our children are not extensions of ourselves but unique souls on their own journeys. As parents, our role is to support, guide, and, ultimately, trust that we have done enough. Parenting becomes an act of faith, a belief that the love we give, the values we instill, and the presence we offer are enough to light their way.

KEY THEMES:

1. **Parenting is Bigger Than Just Raising a Kid:** You're not just taking care of a child; you're shaping the kind of person they'll become. The values you pass on will stick with them, even long after you're gone.
2. **Being There is Half the Battle:** Kids don't need perfect parents. They need present ones. Whether it's five minutes or five hours, being fully there is what makes the difference.
3. **Guide, Don't Control:** Every parent wants to steer their kid in the "right" direction, but trying to control everything only pushes them away. The hardest part? Accepting that they have their own journey, and your job is to guide—not dictate.
4. **Intentional Parenting Takes Effort:** Raising kids isn't just about feeding them and sending them to school. It's about teaching them how to think, how to feel, and how to face the world. That takes patience, empathy, and a lot of deep breaths.

LESSONS AND REFLECTIONS:

This chapter offers reflections on the deep responsibility and beauty of mindful fatherhood:

1. **Karmic Influence:** Recognize that parenthood is not just about the present but about creating a karmic legacy that shapes future generations. Each decision and value imparted carries a ripple effect beyond our own lives.
   1. **Quantum Presence:** Understand that simply being present with your children has a transformative impact. Your presence is a powerful force, one that shapes their sense of self and security in the world.
   2. **Existential Significance:** Acknowledge the weight of parenthood as a path of transcendence, where guiding a child is not just a duty but a spiritual act that outlives your own life.
   3. **Mindful Intention:** Embrace parenting as an act of mindfulness. Be intentional in your interactions, recognizing that every choice you make contributes to the foundation upon which your children will build their lives.

ACTIONABLE STEPS:

To foster mindful, intentional parenting, consider these steps:

1. **Reflect on the Legacy You Want to Leave:** Take time to consider the values and lessons you want to impart. Are you guiding your children to be kind, resilient, and self-aware? Each day, make choices that reflect this legacy.
2. **Practice Presence Daily:** Set aside time each day to be fully present with your children. Whether it's a simple conversation or shared activity, let them know you are there and that they have your attention and your respect.
3. **Embrace the Role of Guide, Not Controller:** Recognize that your children have their own paths to walk. Focus on guiding rather than controlling, and allow them the freedom to make their own choices and learn from them.
4. **Cultivate Patience and Empathy:** Approach each interaction with patience. Respond to their questions, fears, and dreams with empathy, showing them that their thoughts and feelings matter.

CONCLUSION:

There's no perfect way to parent—and anyone who says otherwise is lying. Kids don't need perfection; they need presence. They need parents who show up, who listen, and who teach not just through words but through actions.

You won't always have the right answers. You'll make mistakes. But if your kids know they are loved, if they feel safe to be themselves, you're already doing the most important thing.

In the end, parenting isn't about raising perfect kids—it's about raising kind, thoughtful, strong humans who know they matter.

NINE
EMBRACING SELF-COMPASSION
THE KEY TO LASTING CHANGE

In our pursuit of change, we often mistakenly believe that the journey to success is won through unwavering discipline, self-criticism, and an unyielding determination to improve. We can never achieve transformation by waging an internal war. True change lies in learning to be our own ally, to treat ourselves with the same compassion and understanding we might offer a friend.

The Dalai Lama once said, "If you want others to be happy, practice compassion. If you want to be happy, practice compassion." What he didn't add, perhaps because it is so deeply embedded in his teachings, is that compassion must first be directed inward. Self-compassion is the cornerstone of all compassion; without it, we cannot truly extend kindness to others.

The world teaches us to wear self-criticism as a badge of honor, as though tearing ourselves down will somehow build us up. But think of climbing a mountain with a backpack filled with stones. The weight doesn't make you stronger; it holds you back. But so many of us still carry the weight of self-judgment, regret, and guilt, convinced it's the only way to reach the summit. What if, instead, we lightened the load? What if, instead of punishing ourselves for every slip and stumble, we offered ourselves grace and understanding?

Self-compassion, as the Dalai Lama often reminds us, is not about indulgence. It doesn't mean letting ourselves off the hook or ignoring our mistakes. Instead, it involves treating ourselves with kindness, acknowledging our humanity, and understanding that mistakes are a natural part of our journey.

As the Dalai Lama puts it, "Compassion is the radicalism of our time." Therefore, self-compassion is a form of radical acceptance and a willingness to love ourselves fiercely in a world that often teaches us to do the opposite.

REFLECTIONS ON THE POWER OF SELF-COMPASSION

I used to believe that growth required an unyielding inner critic. I thought that if I didn't hold myself to critical standards, I would never become who I wanted to be and not stand as an example to my team. But every time I fell short, the inner critic grew louder, chaining me to a cycle of judgment and self-doubt. It was like trying to climb with weights tied to my legs. When I finally began to practice self-compassion, I found a different kind of strength, the strength to let go, to forgive, to continue upward without the weight of past mistakes holding me down.

Think about it: if you saw a friend struggling, would you berate them? Would you tell them they were not enough? Of course not. Yet, we do this to ourselves every day. The Dalai Lama has often spoken about this discrepancy, the way we can show boundless compassion to others but withhold it from ourselves. True compassion, he says, begins with kindness toward ourselves. Only then can we extend it outward in a way that is genuine and lasting.

THE PATH OF SELF-FORGIVENESS

Forgiving ourselves is perhaps the most challenging and transformative act of self-compassion. Looking back, I see all the times I acted out of fear, made choices that didn't align with my values, and let the judgments of others guide my path. For years, I couldn't let go of these mistakes. I wore them like scars, convinced they defined me. But as I began to embrace self-compassion, I saw those mistakes for what they truly were: part of my journey, necessary steps that shaped who I am today.

The Dalai Lama teaches that forgiveness, both for ourselves and others, is essential for peace of mind. "Holding on to anger," he says, "is like grasping a hot coal with the intent of throwing it at someone else; you are the one who gets burned." The same is true of self-anger. When we hold on to guilt, shame, and regret, we are the ones who suffer. Forgiveness enables us to release the intense emotions associated with the past, allowing us to fully embrace the present moment.

KEY THEMES:

1. **Self-Compassion as Inner Strength:** Redefine self-compassion as a form of resilience, a path to self-liberation rather than indulgence.
2. **Forgiveness as Release:** Understand forgiveness not as a way to forget but as a way to set ourselves free from the chains of the past.
3. **Radical Acceptance:** Embracing every part of ourselves, including our flaws and mistakes, is integral to our growth.

LESSONS AND REFLECTIONS:

1. **Being Hard on Yourself Won't Get You There Faster:** If beating yourself up actually worked, you'd have everything figured out by now. But it doesn't. Self-criticism doesn't create change—it just drains you. Real growth happens when you learn to support yourself, not constantly tear yourself down.
2. **Forgiveness Starts with You:** Everyone messes up. You, me, all of us. But if you treat guilt like a debt that needs to be repaid, you'll carry that weight forever. Self-forgiveness isn't about forgetting mistakes—it's about learning from them and choosing to move forward instead of staying stuck.
3. **Compassion is Strength, Not Weakness:** The world celebrates hustle, resilience, and pushing through. But the people who truly go the distance? They're not the ones who grind themselves into the ground. They're the ones who know when to slow down, when to rest, and when to give themselves a little grace.
4. **Change Happens in Small Moments:** Nobody wakes up one day as a completely different person. Real transformation isn't

one big moment—it's thousands of small choices. Choosing to pause instead of pushing through exhaustion. Speaking kindly to yourself instead of tearing yourself apart. Letting yourself not have all the answers.

ACTIONABLE STEPS FOR CULTIVATING SELF-COMPASSION:

1. **Challenge Your Inner Critic:** When the voice of self-criticism arises, pause. Ask yourself, "Is this voice helping me, or is it holding me back?" Imagine the Dalai Lama sitting across from you, gently reminding you that self-kindness is not weakness— it's the foundation of true strength. By questioning your inner critic, you weaken its hold.
2. **Practice Self-Forgiveness Daily:** Each day, choose one thing to forgive yourself for, whether it's a small mistake or a long-held regret. Acknowledge the lesson it taught you and then let it go. This daily ritual builds a habit of releasing the past so you can move forward with a lighter heart.
3. **Show Kindness as a Practice**: Compassion is not a one-time act but a continual practice. Treat yourself with kindness in small ways—take a break when you're tired, celebrate small victories, and speak to yourself as you would to a friend. These acts of self-kindness reinforce the habit of compassion.
4. **Reframe Mistakes as Lessons:** The Dalai Lama believes that our flaws are our greatest teachers. Instead of seeing mistakes as failures, view them as lessons. Reflect on what each misstep reveals about your journey and how it guides you toward growth.

CONCLUSION:

The Dalai Lama's teachings remind us that transformation is not about reaching perfection; it's about reaching a place of acceptance. Self-compassion is the foundation that sustains us through life's challenges, allowing us to climb higher without the weight of self-doubt dragging us down. When we forgive ourselves, when we accept our humanity, we build an unshakable inner strength—a strength born not from fighting ourselves but from embracing every part of who we are.

In the end, self-compassion is a quiet, resilient force, a radical choice to be kind to ourselves in a world that demands we be hard. It's the strength that allows us to climb to new heights, to reach further than we ever thought possible, and to look back on our journey—not with regret but with gratitude for every step.

TEN
BUILDING RESILIENCE
NAVIGATING RELATIONSHIPS, SETBACKS, AND THE UNPREDICTABLE

Life is unpredictable. Success and progress often intertwine with failures, setbacks, and challenges. For someone like me, who has been driven by a desire for control and perfection, these moments of uncertainty can feel overwhelming. Yet, my journey has revealed that setbacks are not the end; they are transitions, redirecting us toward growth, resilience, and deeper understanding.

Krishna's guidance to Arjuna in the Mahabharata offers timeless wisdom on navigating such complexities. Arjuna's paralysis on the battlefield wasn't just a reaction to an external war but an internal struggle. Krishna's advice—to act without attachment to outcomes—remains profoundly relevant. It reminds us that resilience is not about erasing chaos but thriving within it, finding meaning in uncertainty, and using it to grow stronger.

REDEFINING FAILURE – A SHIFT IN PERSPECTIVE

Early in my life, I viewed failure as a personal defeat. Setbacks felt like barriers, casting doubt on my abilities and leading me to replay every misstep in my mind. This fear kept me from taking risks and limited my ability to learn from challenges.

Delving into quantum thinking and karma changed my perspective.

Quantum mechanics shows us that reality is filled with possibilities; failure is simply one outcome in a spectrum of potentialities. This shift in thinking helped me see failure not as an endpoint but as an opportunity for recalibration. Similarly, karma teaches us that setbacks are not punishments but the natural consequences of past actions and choices. They offer lessons, providing the chance to reflect and realign.

RESILIENCE IN PARENTING – TEACHING BY EXAMPLE

Parenting has been one of the greatest tests of resilience in my life. My children couldn't be more different from one another. One thrives in structured environments, another seeks freedom and creativity, and yet another mirrors my strengths and vulnerabilities. Their personalities often shift depending on who they are around, but when they interact with me, I see reflections of myself—both the traits I admire and those I strive to change.

My instinct as a father has often been to shield my children from failure. But I've learned that protecting them from hardship denies them the opportunity to build resilience. Instead, I've chosen to guide them through their struggles, teaching them that setbacks are stepping stones, not stumbling blocks. By sharing my failures and how I've navigated them, I aim to show my children that resilience is not about avoiding difficulties but about facing them with courage and learning from them.

FAMILY DYNAMICS – BROTHERS AND THE STRENGTH IN DIFFERENCES

Family relationships have their unique complexities. My elder brother and I think alike, making collaboration easy and fulfilling. My younger brother, on the other hand, brings a very different energy. He is emotional, tactical, and quick to conclusions. Interacting with him requires patience and adaptability—qualities that test and expand my resilience. But the unconditional love our mother has shown to us created a silent bond between us that has stood the test of time. We are there when we need each other, and we are there when others need us.

This dynamic reminds me of the Pandavas in the Mahabharata. Each brother, from Yudhishthira's calm wisdom to Bhima's fiery strength, brought unique qualities that strengthened their collective force. Similarly, I've come to see the differences within my family as assets. While the contrasts can be challenging, they also provide opportunities for growth and deeper understanding.

BALANCING RELATIONSHIPS IN LEADERSHIP – FRIENDS, EMPLOYEES, AND PARTNERS

Leadership often mirrors the complexities of family life. One of my highest-performing employees is a brilliant expert whose inadvertent abrasive demeanor sometimes creates friction within the team. My IT engineers, many of whom are lifelong friends, bring their own personalities, motivations, and challenges to the mix. Balancing these dynamics requires embracing differences while maintaining a shared vision.

Partners add another layer of complexity. Some may act in ways that seem contradictory or self-serving, yet they remain vital to the mission. Navigating these relationships demands patience, empathy, and the resilience to see beyond immediate conflicts.

Elon Musk exemplifies this balance on an extraordinary scale. Leading Tesla, SpaceX, Neuralink, and The Boring Company requires navigating a web of diverse teams, conflicting priorities, and relentless challenges. Musk's ability to pivot, adapt, and focus on long-term goals—despite setbacks—underscores the essence of resilience. His work inspires me to reflect on my ventures and how I strive to create meaningful impact in smaller, more focused ways.

THE INTERSECTION OF RESILIENCE, KARMA, AND GENETICS

Resilience often bridges the divide between what we inherit and what we create. My children's traits reflect a mix of genetics and environment, shaping how they approach challenges. One child's quick temper echoes familial traits, while another's calm introspection feels like a gift passed down through generations.

Karma, in turn, reminds us that our actions shape not just our present but also our future. Together, these forces teach us that while external factors may influence our circumstances, resilience gives us the power to transcend them.

KEY THEMES:

1. **Failure as a Catalyst**: Embracing setbacks as opportunities for growth and transformation rather than endpoints.
2. **Resilience in Relationships**: Balancing family, friends, employees, and partners while navigating conflicts with empathy and purpose.
3. **The Strength of Adaptability**: Pivoting in the face of challenges to find new opportunities and solutions.
4. **Karma and Personal Growth**: Understanding the interplay between past actions and present circumstances to shape a resilient mindset.
5. **Parenting as Leadership**: Modeling resilience for children through authenticity and guidance.

LESSONS AND REFLECTIONS:

1. **Failure is Part of the Game:** You don't get anywhere without setbacks. Success isn't about avoiding failure—it's about what you do after it happens. Do you give up, or do you learn, pivot, and try again? That's what separates people who grow from those who stay stuck.
2. **Relationships Need Space to Breathe:** Whether it's family, friends, or business partners, too much control suffocates a connection. Trust and respect come from allowing people the room to grow, make mistakes, and find their own way.
3. **Parenting Teaches You More Than You Teach Your Kids:** You go into it thinking you're the one guiding them—but then you realize they're teaching you just as much. Patience. Love. The truth about how little control you actually have over anything. It's humbling.
4. **Success Looks Different to Everyone:** The world will tell you what success is—money, titles, recognition. But none of that matters if it doesn't align with what actually fulfills you. Ask yourself: What are you really chasing? And is it even what you want?

ACTIONABLE STEPS FOR BUILDING RESILIENCE

1. **Reframe Failure**: See setbacks as opportunities to learn and grow, not as personal defeats.
2. **Adapt and Pivot**: Stay flexible and open to new directions when plans falter. Innovation often emerges from adversity.
3. **Communicate with Empathy**: In relationships and leadership, practice active listening and open dialogue to build trust and mutual understanding.
4. **Embrace Differences**: Recognize that diversity in personality and perspective strengthens both families and teams.
5. **Focus on the Long Term**: Detach from immediate outcomes and align efforts with a larger purpose, much like Krishna's advice to Arjuna.

CONCLUSION:

Resilience is about embracing life's uncertainties with purpose and grace. Whether managing family dynamics, parenting challenges, or professional setbacks, resilience is the ability to find strength in diversity, meaning in struggle, and clarity in complexity.

As I reflect on Musk's global impact, I find motivation in the parallels to my own journey. While my efforts may not change the trajectory of humanity, they hold significance in the lives I touch—whether through my children, my ventures, or my community. Resilience reminds us that every challenge, every relationship, and every failure is an opportunity to grow, adapt, and make a difference.

Krishna's wisdom teaches us that life's chaos is not something to be feared but embraced. Resilience allows us to navigate this chaos with strength, clarity, and purpose, transforming every setback into a stepping stone toward our greatest potential.

ELEVEN
CULTIVATING INNER PEACE
NAVIGATING THE CHAOS WITH STILLNESS

Having journeyed through impulsivity, communication, love, parenting, self-compassion, and resilience, I find myself drawn to a pursuit that feels both deceptively simple and profoundly elusive: inner peace. Amid the relentless chaos of life, balancing the demands of business, family, personal growth, and love, finding stillness has become not only a challenge but also a necessity. Through my experiences, I've come to realize that inner peace and chaos are not opposing forces but companions that must coexist.

Chaos is a constant, regardless of age or circumstance. I've seen it in the lives of my children, where the moment they are given choices and exposed to restrictive thinking, chaos begins. As parents, we often impose our views on our children without considering their perspectives. I've done the same. Early on, I thought it was my responsibility to steer their lives, to decide what they should learn and which paths they should take. But as I've matured in both my role as a parent and a leader, I've come to understand that objective persuasion is far more effective than forced, subjective pushes.

Leaders like Elon Musk and Steve Jobs exemplify how the balance of chaos and inner peace plays out on a larger stage. Musk, while lauded for his groundbreaking ventures like Tesla, SpaceX, and Neuralink, often displays behavior that leans into chaos. His relentless work ethic, which reportedly includes micromanagement and fiery outbursts, has created tension among his teams.

Musk's focus on innovation sometimes comes at the expense of his relationships, both personal and professional. Yet, when he approaches challenges with clarity and vision, detaching from immediate setbacks to focus on long-term goals, he demonstrates a form of leadership that cultivates progress and, perhaps, moments of inner peace.

Steve Jobs, on the other hand, was a master of compartmentalization. Known for his intense personality and high expectations, Jobs often clashed with his colleagues, creating environments of both brilliance and burnout. His early years at Apple were marked by impulsivity and a lack of empathy, which led to conflicts and even his removal from the company.

However, his time away from Apple allowed him to reflect and grow. When he returned, Jobs channeled his intensity more effectively, focusing on clear, deliberate decisions that aligned with his vision for innovation. While he may not have epitomized inner peace, his ability to evolve and balance his behavior illustrates the transformative power of self-awareness and intentional action.

As a parent, I've learned that chaos is inevitable. My children, with their unique personalities and perspectives, often challenge my assumptions and force me to reflect on my approach. In these moments, I've found that consciously choosing how to respond rather than reacting impulsively is key to maintaining inner peace. This is not about suppressing chaos but about navigating it with clarity and grace.

The same principles apply to leadership. A simple argument with a coworker can create a ripple effect, spilling over into your personal life. I've experienced this firsthand. On days when I compartmentalized work issues and left them at the office, I felt a disconnect that ultimately impacted my interactions with family. Conversely, carrying personal frustrations into the workplace altered my professional demeanor, creating unnecessary tension. Inner peace requires conscious living—a deliberate effort to separate and address various aspects of life without allowing them to bleed into one another.

Conscious living involves acknowledging the chaos and choosing to approach it with intention. This means setting boundaries, managing expectations, and cultivating self-awareness. It's about creating a mental space where both chaos and stillness can coexist, where external turbulence doesn't dictate internal calm.

Inner peace is directly linked to happiness, which is, ultimately, the goal of life. Happiness isn't the absence of conflict or challenge but the ability to find meaning and contentment amidst them. This realization has reshaped how I approach both parenting and leadership.

As I guide my children and my teams, I've learned that my behavior, shaped by conscious living, sets the tone for those around me. Whether it's through objective persuasion with my children or empathetic leadership with my teams, the way I handle chaos influences not just my inner peace but also the harmony of my environment.

Quantum mechanics provides an apt metaphor for this balance. Just as particles exist in a state of potential until observed, our lives hold the potential for both chaos and calm. The state we embody depends on where we direct our focus. By observing my thoughts and emotions without judgment, I've learned to cultivate inner stillness even in turbulent moments. This doesn't mean ignoring the chaos; it means embracing it as a natural part of life while choosing not to be overwhelmed by it.

Karma also plays a pivotal role in this journey. The actions, intentions, and energy we put into the world shape our experiences. Approaching life with kindness, patience, and acceptance creates a karmic environment conducive to inner harmony. In contrast, reacting impulsively or holding on to control generates turbulence. Inner peace is not a passive state; it's an active process of aligning actions and intentions with the values we wish to embody.

Inner peace, I've found, is contagious. When I approach life with stillness and clarity, it ripples outward, influencing my interactions with others. My children are more receptive, my teams collaborate more effectively, and my personal relationships thrive. Chaos may never disappear, but the way I navigate it determines the quality of my inner world and the environments I create.

KEY THEMES:

1. **Inner Peace and Chaos Are Two Sides of the Same Coin:** Most people think peace means eliminating chaos—but the truth is, both exist at the same time. The real skill isn't avoiding chaos—it's learning how to stay grounded in the middle of it.
2. **Parenting and Leadership Require Conscious Living:** Whether you're leading a team or raising kids, it's a constant balancing act. You have to guide without controlling, teach

without forcing, and respect individuality while still providing structure.
3. **Managing Stress with Boundaries:** If you don't separate work from home, or personal from professional, stress will seep into every part of your life. Compartmentalization isn't avoidance—it's about keeping things in their right place so one struggle doesn't take over everything.
4. **Happiness and Inner Peace Are Choices:** Neither happens by accident. Peace isn't something you stumble upon—it's something you create through intentional decisions, mindset shifts, and daily actions.
5. **Even the Greatest Minds Wrestle with Chaos:** Leaders like Elon Musk and Steve Jobs didn't succeed because their lives were peaceful—they succeeded because they learned how to function within the chaos, using it as fuel rather than letting it consume them.

LESSONS AND REFLECTIONS:

1. **Peace Isn't Something You "Find":** It's not waiting for you at the end of a vacation, a perfect paycheck, or the right relationship. If you can't find peace in the middle of chaos, you won't find it anywhere.
2. **Slowing Down is a Power Move:** Society glorifies constant movement, but the people who actually achieve the most know when to stop, breathe, and think. Pausing isn't weakness—it's strategy.
3. **Your Mind Creates the Storm or the Stillness:** Two people can be in the exact same situation—one feels overwhelmed, the other feels calm. The difference? How they choose to see it. Your mindset dictates your experience more than the situation itself.
4. **Not Every Battle is Worth Fighting:** Some arguments are just distractions. Some problems solve themselves if you stop feeding them attention. Part of peace is knowing when to walk away and save your energy for what really matters.

ACTIONABLE STEPS:

1. **Practice Objective Persuasion**: In both parenting and leadership, approach challenges with empathy and rationality rather than force.
2. **Set Boundaries**: Separate your work and personal lives by addressing issues within their contexts to prevent unnecessary spillover.
3. **Cultivate Mindfulness**: Observe thoughts and emotions without judgment, creating a space for calm amidst chaos.
4. **Align with Values**: Act with kindness, patience, and acceptance to foster inner and outer harmony.
5. **Learn from Leaders**: Reflect on the examples of Musk and Jobs, adopting effective practices and learning from their mistakes.

CONCLUSION:

Life won't slow down for you. Chaos isn't going anywhere. But inner peace? That's something you can build no matter what's happening around you.

It's not about waiting for the "right" time to relax or hoping for a stress-free life. It's about learning to find calm even in the middle of the storm.

Some days will be harder than others. You'll lose your footing, get caught up in things that don't matter, and forget to take a breath. That's okay. The goal isn't perfection—it's progress.

Keep coming back to yourself. Keep finding the quiet spaces, even when everything else is loud. That's where peace really lives.

TWELVE
THE POWER OF GRATITUDE
SHIFTING FOCUS TO ABUNDANCE

A s I've navigated the complexities of life—balancing the roles of father, business leader, partner, and an individual striving for growth—I've come to understand one profound truth: perspective shapes reality. In the face of setbacks, chaos, and daily struggles, it's all too easy to be consumed by what's lacking, what's wrong, or what isn't enough. For much of my life, I fell into this trap, endlessly chasing external validation and success, only to feel empty once I achieved it. Gratitude changed everything.

Gratitude, I've learned, is not just a fleeting feeling or a polite thank-you. It's a lens through which we can view life, transforming scarcity into abundance, complaint into appreciation, and despair into hope. It's not about ignoring challenges but about finding meaning within them.

In this chapter, I reflect on how cultivating gratitude has become the cornerstone of my journey, allowing me to reconnect with myself, strengthen my relationships, and embrace the unpredictable nature of life.

REDEFINING SUCCESS THROUGH GRATITUDE

For years, I equated success with external achievements—business milestones, financial stability, accolades, and status symbols. Yet, no matter how much I achieved, fulfillment felt like a mirage. Each goal I reached was quickly replaced by the desire for the next, leaving me in a constant state of dissatisfaction.

I remember moments when I should have felt on top of the world, such as after closing a business deal, receiving recognition, or reaching a milestone. Instead, I felt hollow, chasing a future that always seemed just out of reach. The cycle was exhausting, and it robbed me of the ability to appreciate what was already mine.

This relentless pursuit began to shift as I explored the principles of quantum thinking and karma. I started to see success not as something external but as an internal state of being. Success, I realized, isn't about what you achieve but about how you engage with life. Gratitude became my gateway to this new perspective.

Gratitude taught me that true wealth lies in the present moment. It's in the laughter of my children, the lessons hidden in setbacks, and the quiet beauty of everyday life. By shifting my focus from outcomes to experiences, from scarcity to abundance, I discovered a sense of fulfillment that doesn't depend on external circumstances. Gratitude redefined success for me, transforming it from a source of stress into a source of peace.

QUANTUM THINKING AND THE ENERGY OF GRATITUDE

Quantum mechanics teaches us that energy follows focus. Just as particles change their behavior when observed, our internal state transforms when we choose what to focus on. Gratitude is a powerful focal point that shifts energy toward positivity and abundance.

When frustration or doubt creeps in, gratitude serves as a grounding force. Instead of being overwhelmed by what's wrong, I intentionally direct my focus toward what's right. It's not about pretending life is perfect but about acknowledging the gifts hidden within challenges. This shift creates space for joy, peace, and contentment.

I've found that gratitude changes the state of my experience. By observing life through this lens, I uncover opportunities and possibilities that once seemed obscured by negativity. It's a reminder that abundance isn't about having more; it's about seeing more.

THE KARMIC CYCLE OF GRATITUDE

Gratitude isn't just an internal practice; it has karmic implications. When I express gratitude through words, actions, or even thoughts, I create positive energy that ripples outward. This energy not only shapes my internal state but also influences my relationships and environments.

Gratitude has transformed my dynamic with my children. Instead of focusing on what they could do better, I consciously acknowledge their strengths, efforts, and the joy they bring into my life. This shift fosters trust, openness, and connection, allowing them to feel seen and valued.

In my professional life, gratitude has strengthened my relationships with colleagues and partners. Expressing appreciation for their contributions creates a culture of respect and collaboration. When gratitude becomes a shared value, it fosters loyalty and trust, turning work into a space of mutual growth rather than competition.

DAILY PRACTICES FOR CULTIVATING GRATITUDE

Gratitude is a practice, not a destination. It requires consistency and effort, especially in the face of life's challenges. Here are some practices that have become integral to my journey:

1. **Gratitude Journaling:** Each day, I write down three things I'm grateful for. They can be as simple as a warm meal or as profound as a meaningful conversation. This practice shifts my focus toward abundance and reminds me that even on hard days, there is something to celebrate.
2. **Expressing Appreciation:** I make a conscious effort to thank those around me, from my children to my team. Verbalizing gratitude strengthens bonds and reinforces the habit of seeing the good in others.
3. **Reframing Challenges:** When faced with setbacks, I challenge myself to find one thing to be grateful for. It could be lessons learned, resilience built, or new perspectives gained. This reframing transforms resistance into acceptance.
4. **Gratitude Meditation:** During meditation, I focus on the feeling of gratitude, reflecting on the people, experiences, and

opportunities that have enriched my life. This anchors me in the present and cultivates peace.

THE TRANSFORMATIVE POWER OF GRATITUDE

Gratitude has transformed how I perceive challenges, interact with others, and approach each day. It has taught me that abundance isn't about accumulating more but about appreciating what already exists. This shift has empowered me to face life's unpredictability with grace, knowing that there is light even in the darkest moments.

In relationships, gratitude fosters deeper connections. When I express appreciation for my children, colleagues, or partner, I create a foundation of trust, empathy, and love. This practice strengthens bonds, encourages open communication, and nurtures positivity in all areas of life.

KEY THEMES:

1. **Gratitude Shifts Focus from Scarcity to Abundance:** When you focus on what's missing, life feels like a constant chase. But when you focus on what's already there, everything shifts. Gratitude isn't just about feeling good—it's about seeing life differently.
2. **Redefining Success Through Gratitude:** Real success isn't just about reaching goals—it's about finding peace in the process. Gratitude helps reframe what truly matters, reminding you that achievement means nothing without appreciation.
3. **The Quantum and Karmic Power of Gratitude:** What you focus on expands. Quantum thinking suggests that our attention shapes reality, and karma ensures that the energy we put out returns to us. Gratitude amplifies both, creating a cycle of positivity.
4. **Gratitude Strengthens Relationships and Personal Growth:** Expressing appreciation—not just feeling it—deepens connections and builds trust. It turns everyday interactions into moments of meaning and reminds you of the richness in your life.

LESSONS AND REFLECTIONS:

1. **You See What You Focus On:** If you're always searching for what's missing, that's all you'll find. But the moment you start recognizing what's already in front of you, your entire perspective changes.
2. **Gratitude is a Daily Practice, Not a One-Time Fix:** Feeling thankful once in a while is easy. Training your mind to find gratitude every single day? That's what rewires your thinking and shifts your reality.
3. **Abundance Isn't About Having More:** More money, more success, more status—it never actually makes you feel full. Real abundance comes from realizing that what you have right now is already enough.
4. **Giving Back Expands What You Have:** The more you share, the more you realize how much you already possess. Gratitude isn't just about receiving—it's about acknowledging, appreciating, and passing it forward.

ACTIONABLE STEPS:

1. **Keep a Gratitude Journal:** Every day, write down three things you're thankful for—big or small. Over time, this simple habit rewires your brain to focus on what's present rather than what's missing.
2. **Say It Out Loud:** Don't just think about your gratitude—express it. Call, text, or tell someone in person that you appreciate them. It strengthens relationships and reinforces positive energy in both of you.
3. **Find the Silver Lining in a Challenge:** Look at something that's frustrating or difficult right now. Instead of focusing on what's wrong, ask yourself: Is there anything in this situation to be grateful for? A lesson? A hidden opportunity? A moment of growth?
4. **Reflect in Stillness:** Spend five minutes in quiet meditation or deep thought, focusing on the people, experiences, and moments that bring meaning to your life. Let gratitude ground you in the present.

CONCLUSION:

Gratitude is more than an emotion; it's a way of being. It's the conscious choice to embrace life with an attitude of abundance and appreciation. By cultivating gratitude, I shift my focus from what's lacking to what's present, from what's wrong to what's beautiful. This practice grounds me in the present moment, connects me to the people around me, and fills my life with a sense of joy and purpose.

Living a life of gratitude opens the door to endless possibilities. It's not about ignoring life's chaos but about navigating it with a heart full of appreciation. Gratitude reminds me that every experience, whether joyful or challenging, adds to the richness of life.

THIRTEEN
MANIFESTING INTENTIONS
TURNING THOUGHT INTO REALITY

As I progress on my journey of self-awareness, emotional growth, and intentional living, I find myself increasingly drawn to the power of intention. It's an idea that bridges the spiritual and scientific realms, rooted in the understanding that our thoughts, beliefs, and focus have the ability to shape our reality. You don't "manifest" anything. You work, sweat, fail, and try again. That's the only way things happen. It's a practice of creating, not controlling—a dance between effort and surrender.

CLARITY AS THE FOUNDATION OF MANIFESTATION

In my earlier years, I lived as though ambition alone could shape my life. I chased goals society deemed important—career achievements, financial stability, and outward recognition—without questioning if they aligned with my true desires. This scattered pursuit left me chasing outcomes that often felt hollow. I would achieve one milestone, only to feel compelled to move on to the next, with no real sense of fulfillment.

Manifestation starts with clarity. What truly matters to you in life and why? This question became the foundation of my life. Instead of being overwhelmed by impulsive desires or societal expectations, I genuinely learned to pause and reflect. My current aspirations aren't random ambitions. They're aligned with my core values and filled with an important and meaningful purpose.

Clarity allows me to focus my energy on where it matters. It's like planting a seed: the more precise I am about what I want to grow, the better I can nurture it. When I set a clear intention, I guide not just my actions but my thoughts, emotions, and decisions. This helps create a sense of purpose that permeates every aspect of my life.

QUANTUM THINKING: THE SCIENCE OF MANIFESTATION

Jiddu Krishnamurti never spoke about quantum mechanics, yet his teachings align with its core mystery—**that observation changes reality.** He believed that **pure awareness, without judgment, transforms the way we think and act.**

In physics, **the double-slit experiment** reveals that **particles behave like waves—until they are observed, at which point they "choose" a definite state.** In life, Krishnamurti argued that **self-awareness does the same thing**—shining a light on unconscious patterns, forcing them to take shape.

This connects directly to manifestation. The excerpt states:

> *"When we look at ourselves in the third person, our behavior dramatically changes to what is right. The act of focusing on an intention shapes the outcomes we experience in life."*

- **Quantum physics shows that focused attention determines reality.**
- **Krishnamurti taught that watching yourself changes your behavior.**
- **Manifestation works by directing thought and energy toward a specific outcome.**

Krishnamurti didn't need science to prove his point—**he simply understood that where attention goes, reality follows.**

This isn't about magical thinking. Manifestation is rooted in the conscious alignment of thought and action. For example, if I set an intention to foster deeper connections with my children, my energy naturally shifts toward seeking opportunities for bonding. I experienced this in real life. Whether it's setting aside work to have a meaningful conversation or simply being present during dinner, my actions align with my intention. If we have a deeply rooted desire for any outcome, more likely than not, we experience that outcome. This creates a feedback loop where the bond grows stronger, reinforcing the original vision.

It's not the thought alone that changes reality; it's the focus and action that follow. Manifestation requires strong discipline, unwavering clarity, and a willingness to work in harmony with the energy of intention—**just like a gardener tending to a seed.**

A gardener doesn't simply drop a seed in the ground and expect it to flourish overnight. **They prepare the soil, making sure it has the right nutrients. They choose the right environment, knowing that some seeds thrive in sunlight while others need shade.** Once planted, the seed must be watered regularly, but not drowned; protected, but not shielded so much that it never adapts.

And most importantly? **The gardener understands that growth takes time.** They don't dig up the seed every day to check if it's sprouting. They trust the unseen work happening beneath the surface, knowing that, with patience and care, roots will take hold before anything visible appears.

Manifestation works the same way. **A single thought isn't enough.** You have to cultivate it, nurture it, and **create the right conditions for it to take shape.** Some desires materialize quickly, like fast-growing herbs, while others, like oak trees, take years. The key is **consistent effort, belief in the process, and the patience to allow things to unfold in their own time.**

KARMA: ALIGNING ACTIONS WITH INTENTIONS

Manifestation and karma are intrinsically linked. Karma, the principle of cause and effect, teaches us that the quality of our actions determines the quality of our outcomes. Manifestation works similarly: intentions must be paired with actions that align with the energy of those desires.

If my intention is to build a purpose-driven company, I cannot act out of greed or dishonesty and expect positive results. Integrity, hard work, and perseverance are essential. The actions I take must reflect the values of the outcome I seek. Misaligned actions—driven by fear, doubt, or impatience —generate chaos rather than clarity.

This understanding of karma has reshaped how I approach manifestation. I now focus not just on the destination but on the path I take to get there. Every step matters. Every action contributes to the karmic energy that supports—or hinders—the realization of my goals.

PRACTICES FOR MANIFESTING INTENTIONS

Manifesting intentions isn't a simple, one-time event but a consistently practiced and trust-based act. Here are the tools that have helped me turn thought into reality:

1. **Visualization:** Each morning, I spend time visualizing my intentions as if they've already manifested. I imagine the sights, sounds, and emotions of achieving that goal. Visualization anchors my focus and creates a sense of alignment between my thoughts and actions.
2. **Affirmations:** Repeating affirmations grounds my intentions in daily life. Regular and repeated statements like "I am building meaningful relationships with my children" or "I am creating a company that reflects my values" serve as reminders to stay aligned with my goals.
3. **Aligned Actions:** Manifestation is not passive. For every intention, I identify specific actions that will move me closer to it. Whether it's setting aside time for family or refining a business plan, consistently aligned action turns intention into reality.
4. **Letting Go:** The most challenging part of manifestation is releasing attachment to the outcome. I have learned to focus on the process, trusting that the universe will unfold my intentions in ways that might even surpass my original vision.
5. **Gratitude:** Gratitude amplifies manifestation by shifting my focus from scarcity to abundance. It reminds me that I am already equipped with the resources, experiences, and energy to bring my intentions to life.

MANIFESTATION IN RELATIONSHIPS

Intentions are not limited to career or personal growth; they extend into relationships. If I wish to deepen my bond with my children, my behavior must reflect that desire. Listening more, being present, and expressing appreciation are actions that align with the intention of connection.

Simple acts like donuts with dads are as important as celebrating a birthday party.

In romantic relationships, manifesting love requires self-reflection. Am I being the partner I want to attract? Am I embodying honesty, empathy, and respect? Manifestation in relationships is not about finding the right person but about becoming the person who resonates with the love I seek.

BALANCING INTENTION AND ACCEPTANCE

Manifestation isn't about controlling outcomes; it's about creating alignment. There are moments when, despite my best efforts, life takes an unexpected turn. These moments remind me that manifestation requires both focus and surrender. While I can influence reality through intention, I must also trust in the flow of life. This does not necessarily mean that we make the right choices. I can make a wrong choice, manifest the choice, and bear the outcome.

This balance between intention and acceptance mirrors the principles of quantum thinking and karma. Outcomes, whether they match my vision or not, carry valuable lessons. Manifestation is not just about achieving goals; it's about embracing the journey.

KEY THEMES:

1. **Clarity and Alignment Create the Foundation for Manifestation:** Before anything can become real, you have to know exactly what you want—and that means aligning your thoughts, actions, and emotions with that vision. Without clarity, manifestation is just wishful thinking.
2. **Focused Thought Shapes Reality:** Quantum physics tells us that what we observe, we influence. Our thoughts, when focused and intentional, have a way of shaping the world around us—sometimes in ways we don't even realize.
3. **Karma Connects Intention, Action, and Outcome:** Manifestation isn't just about wanting something—it's about what you do to bring it to life. Every action plants a seed, and karma ensures that what you put out will eventually return.
4. **Balance Between Effort and Surrender:** There's a fine line between working toward something and forcing it. The best

manifestations happen when you take action but also trust that life unfolds in its own time.

LESSONS AND REFLECTIONS:

1. **Manifestation is More Than Just Thinking About What You Want:** It's not enough to hope or visualize. Your thoughts need to be backed by action, consistency, and belief.
2. **Not Everything Will Go as Planned—And That's Okay:** You can set an intention and do everything "right," but life has a way of surprising you. Sometimes, the outcome is better than what you originally wanted—if you're open to seeing it.
3. **Your Energy Affects What You Attract:** The energy you bring into situations—whether it's desperation, confidence, or fear—shapes what you experience in return. The clearer and calmer you are, the smoother things flow.

ACTIONABLE STEPS:

1. Spend five minutes daily visualizing a clear intention as though it has already manifested.
2. Create affirmations that reflect your deepest desires and repeat them each morning.
3. Identify one aligned action you can take today to bring your intention closer to reality.
4. Practice gratitude for the steps you've taken and the journey ahead, reinforcing the energy of abundance.

CONCLUSION:

Manifesting intentions is an act of empowerment. It's a practice that allows you to take an active role in shaping your reality while remaining open to the unexpected. By aligning thoughts, actions, and energy with your desires, you create a life that reflects your deepest values and aspirations.

This process is not about controlling every detail of existence. It's about guiding your journey with clarity, trust, and purpose. Manifestation, at its core, is a dance between focus and flow, effort and surrender. It's about holding a vision in your heart while navigating life with the understanding that every moment contributes to the unfolding of that vision.

FOURTEEN
EMBRACING CHANGE
NAVIGATING LIFE'S TRANSITIONS WITH GRACE

Life is an endless journey of continuous Change. For me, some instances of change have been so intense and sudden that they felt like stab wounds that may never fully heal. Others were gentler, pushing me in a new direction. Some changes have caused me to question my very existence on this planet, while others have awakened a fire in me to grow, adapt, and rebuild.

Change doesn't come in neatly prescribed packages. It arrives uninvited and in all forms, like a child leaving home, a friendship ending, or the collapse of a once solidly stable economy. It also could be the thrill of finding a new partner or even the bitterness of realizing that someone undeserving has risen to a position of absolute power. Change could even be the societal shifts caused by technological revolutions, like artificial intelligence or cryptocurrencies, disrupting industries, reshaping wealth, and impacting life. Each shift challenges us, forcing us to decide who we are and what we are becoming.

PERSONAL BATTLES OF CHANGE

Some changes have shaken me to my core. The departure of loved ones, changes in relationships, and the realization that time has no sympathy have all forced me to confront myself. As my children grew and transitioned into their adult lives, I felt satisfied and also a strange sense of loss. Parenting shifted from being hands-on to becoming a quiet support system, creating a void in my daily routines.

The external world doesn't pause for your personal chaos. There's always a profound battle within us to grow, adapt, and remain relevant. Careers evolve to new heights or bog down in irrelevance. Friends may come and go, with new circles emerging or you being left alone, with each bringing its own joys and complexities. The social circles I once belonged to now feel as distant as politics. Personal priorities and life circumstances often pull people in different directions.

Then there's a bigger context. Watching the world around you change, with wars erupting, political corruption proliferating, and a wide variety of global conflicts unfolding based on religion, the personal agendas of leaders, and greed, adds another layer of uncertainty. The rise of AI and the financial disruptions of crypto and blockchain technologies have greatly redefined wealth and the balance of power. These forces are creating both opportunities and challenges, leaving us to ponder how we fit into this new, ever-changing world.

CHANGE AS A CATALYST FOR GROWTH

While some changes feel like major damage, more often than not, they pave the way for something new. It is human nature to resist change, to cling to what is familiar. But if we want to grow, we must let go of that fear, shed the layers of comfort found in the known, and embrace the chaos of the unknown.

Famous figures throughout history have struggled with change. Take Steve Jobs, who faced being ousted from the company he founded. That moment of humiliation and the loss became the seed for one of the greatest comebacks ever seen. He used the space created by that disruptive change to innovate further, building one of the world's most iconic companies, Pixar, and laying the groundwork for his eventual return to Apple, where he further redefined the technology landscape in a way no one had ever seen.

On the flip side, change doesn't always lead to immediate success. Elon Musk, with his ventures in Tesla, SpaceX, and Neuralink, symbolizes the relentless pursuit of a vision amid constant disruption. His life is a testament to navigating chaos, criticism, financial losses, and the ever-present risk of failure. Musk thrives in the chaos, using it as fuel for his larger-than-life ambitions. Yet, even he admits the damage it causes to personal relationships and mental health, showing that change, while a big driver of progress, comes with some sacrifices.

THE EMOTIONAL TOLL OF TRANSITION

Change, more times than not, isn't just external; it's deeply personal. There were many moments in my life when I felt as though the ground under me had vanished. Losing critical connections, facing unimagined betrayals, and adapting to new emerging realities forced me to reevaluate my purpose and strength. As I age, these transitions have not been any easier. If anything, they keep getting harder, as I'm burdened by experience and the realization that time is finite.

The most difficult part of change is its randomness. One day, you feel like you are on top of the world, and the next, you are brought to your knees by an unexpected loss or challenge. Navigating these random, unpredictable shifts requires not just mental strength but a willingness to accept that control is an illusion.

LESSONS FROM LEADERS AND LEGENDS

Throughout history, great leaders have faced some amazing transformative moments that re-defined their legacies. Think of Mahatma Gandhi's decision to lead India's independence movement through nonviolence. It was not just a political change that was different from others but a deeply personal one, perhaps a questionable one, which required him to abandon the comforts and immerse himself in the freedom struggle. His remarkable ability to transform the constant chaos of a revolution into a transformative vision of peace and justice continues to captivate and inspire generations.

In mythology, Krishna's guidance to Arjuna in the Mahabharata exemplifies the wisdom required to embrace change. Arjuna was paralyzed, torn between duty and emotion, unable to take action amidst transformation. Krishna's counsel—to concentrate on the action and release the outcome—provides timeless advice on gracefully navigating transitions.

FINDING STRENGTH AMID CHANGE

Navigating change demands resilience, which is cultivated through perspective. I've realized that change isn't inherently good or bad; its impact depends on our response. When I stopped resisting change and embraced it, I discovered opportunities for growth that seemed unimaginable.

Mindfulness has become my anchor during turbulent transitions. By focusing on the present moment, I can ground myself even when the future appears uncertain. Gratitude has also proven to be a potent tool. In times of upheaval, I've learned to appreciate the small things to be thankful for— a supportive conversation, a new opportunity, or simply the resilience to face another day.

THE RIPPLE EFFECT OF CHANGE

Change doesn't just impact us individually; it ripples outward and inward, influencing our relationships with the workplace, friends and family, careers, and communities. As a father, I've seen how my children's phases of growth have impacted my own. Their transitions challenge me to adjust as a parent to new realities, cease the micro control, and trust their journey.

In the professional space, change often creates tension as employees question their trust in their leaders. I've managed teams during industry disruptions, all the way from the rise of AI to economic downturns, and each disruptive change has required a unique balancing act with innovation. Witnessing employees struggle to adapt, partners betray expectations, and friends drifting away due to ever-changing priorities has taught me to approach change with utmost empathy. Everyone experiences change differently, and understanding this has helped me navigate transitions with compassion.

KEY THEMES:

1. **Change is the Only Constant:** Life never stays still. No matter how much we resist it, change is always happening— sometimes gradually, sometimes all at once. The sooner we accept that, the easier it becomes to grow.
2. **Lessons from History, Myths, and Legends:** We're not the first to face major transitions. Myths, famous figures, and past generations have left us clues about how to handle change with wisdom and resilience.
3. **Adapting to Change Affects More Than Just You:** Whether it's personal, professional, or relational, change

doesn't happen in isolation. Understanding its emotional impact on yourself and those around you makes all the difference.
4. **Mindfulness and Gratitude Make Transitions Easier:** Instead of clinging to what's slipping away, focusing on the present moment and what's still in your control helps you navigate uncertainty with less stress and more clarity.

LESSONS AND REFLECTIONS:

1. **Change Never Feels Good at First:** Even when it's leading you somewhere better, the beginning of change almost always feels uncomfortable. That discomfort isn't a sign that something's wrong—it's proof that you're growing.
2. **You Can't Plan Everything:** No matter how detailed your five-year plan is, life will throw unexpected detours at you. Some of the best things in life come from the moments you never saw coming.
3. **Resisting Change Only Makes It Harder:** The more you fight against change, the more exhausting and painful it becomes. The second you accept it and start moving forward, the weight of resistance starts to lift.
4. **The People Who Adapt, Thrive:** Some people get stuck in the past and let it define them. Others embrace what's ahead and create new opportunities. Which kind of person do you want to be?

ACTIONABLE STEPS:

1. Reflect on a significant life change. What did it reveal about your true self?
2. Identify a grounding practice, like journaling or deep breathing, to help you stay centered during transitions.
3. Approach the next change with curiosity instead of resistance.
4. Learn from past experiences to guide your response to future challenges.

CONCLUSION:

Change is not an enemy to be defeated but a necessity to be embraced. It strips away the excess and unrequired and challenges us to become something different. At the core of its unpredictability, it teaches us to be adaptable, focus on what really matters, and trust the unfolding of life's journey.

Whether it's the chaos of a shifting world, the disruption in personal relationships, or the transformation of industries, change is constant and inevitable. What matters is how and where we meet it, with resistance or with grace, with fear or with curiosity. As I continue my journey of life, I firmly believe that change, even if it's disruptive, presents an opportunity for personal growth and alignment. It's a chance to step closer to the authentic version of myself and become the person I'm meant to be.

FIFTEEN
THE ART OF BEING PRESENT
CULTIVATING MINDFULNESS IN EVERY MOMENT

Life's fading moments have a way of slipping past us, often unnoticed. Eventually, they become distant memories we long to revisit or are reminded of by the participants of those moments. Reflecting on my journey of embracing change, building resilience, manifesting intentions, and finding inner peace, I realize that all these practices depend on one transformative ability: being fully present. Developing mindfulness has become not just a choice but a necessity for living a meaningful life in a world overflowing with distractions and demands.

THE RELENTLESS CHASE AND ITS INVISIBLE COST

For years, I was stuck in a relentless pursuit of achievements and milestones, convinced that they would eventually bring me happiness. This mindset fueled my ambition, but it came at a significant cost. I recall the day I missed "Donuts with Dads" at my kid's school despite my son reminding me repeatedly, going instead to a last-minute, "urgent" work meeting.

At the time, his request seemed small and an everyday non-event, while the meeting felt big. In retrospect, the pain of my child's disappointment when he couldn't find me in the room and his lost opportunity to share one of life's simple joys overshadowed any professional gain I may have achieved. Seemingly insignificant events like this one can collectively create a deep scar that could affect and shape his adult behavior.

Even family vacations, meant to be memorable escapes to build togetherness, became opportunities for work to intervene. I would leave my kids by the pool while I caught up on emails, telling myself that this sacrifice was necessary and that my job helped fund these moments. But the irony was blatant. Though physically present, I was mentally absent, missing the joy unfolding around me, and their constant requests to join the fun were buried under my repeated response: "Let me answer this, and then I will be there."

These painful, personal moments serve as a reminder of the choices made by famous leaders like Elon Musk and Steve Jobs. Musk's relentless pursuit of innovation has revolutionized industries, but he has acknowledged the toll this intensity has taken on his personal relationships.

Similarly, Steve Jobs, well known for his visionary genius, faced criticism for the emotional detachment he maintained during critical periods of his life. However, as he progressed in his journey of life, Jobs became more deliberate about his relationships, choosing to prioritize personal moments with his family.

These stories are not simply random tales but profound lessons that deeply resonate with my struggle to balance ambition with the importance of being present.

THE KARMIC CYCLE OF DISENGAGEMENT

The karmic consequences of life absences are profound. When we prioritize work, ambition, or even fleeting distractions over genuine human connections, we set in motion a notorious, regrettable cycle of absence. Children who grow up feeling disconnected from their parents often repeat these same patterns, chasing external validation instead of building meaningful relationships.

I see this cycle well reflected in my own life. Despite recognizing the weight of missed moments, I found myself repeating similar behaviors, thinking about work or engaging in any other trivial activity while kids shared stories from school or letting my work worries cloud moments meant for joy.

It's a brutal irony that even when we know better, breaking the pattern feels challenging. The truth is that without mindfulness, the karmic cycle of disconnect only deepens.

QUANTUM PRESENCE – SHAPING REALITY THROUGH ATTENTION

We learn from quantum mechanics that observation changes reality. In life, where our attention is focused determines our experiences. Presence becomes a form of quantum observation that deeply affects our relationships, decisions, and inner peace.

When I actively choose to be present in a conversation with my child, during a team discussion, or while enjoying a personal moment, there's a noticeable shift. The noise of distractions quickly fades, and clarity quickly emerges, resulting in a much fuller and richer experience. Being present is not just a philosophical concept; it's a tangible reality. It transforms not only how we perceive life but also how life unfolds around us.

For leaders, this key principle is equally transformative. Steve Jobs famously said that "focus means saying no to a thousand things," an idea that applies to mindfulness as much as it does to innovation. Jobs developed an ability to focus his attention on what mattered most, whether perfecting a product or spending time with family, which became a defining aspect of his legacy.

In my life, practicing presence has reminded me that success is not just about how much we do but about the depth with which we engage in those activities.

PRACTICING MINDFULNESS IN DAILY LIFE

Mindfulness requires more intention than perfection. Below are some of the practices that have helped me reclaim presence in the chaos of an ever-changing life:

Mindful Breathing: When stress or distraction threatens to overwhelm me, I pause to focus on my breath. This simple act serves as a crucial grounding mechanism, redirecting my attention to the present moment.

Gratitude Reflection: Each day, I take time to reflect on three instances that brought me joy or cultivated a sense of connection. These moments often reveal the beauty that can be easily overlooked amid the rush of day-to-day life.

Purposeful Listening: In conversations, I intentionally set aside my thoughts to fully engage with the other person. This practice has not only improved my understanding of what is being said but also strengthened my emotional connection with the speaker.

Boundaries with Technology: Whether I'm enjoying a meal with my family or participating in a team meeting, I consciously make an effort to put away my devices and fully immerse myself in the present moment.

THE RIPPLE EFFECT OF PRESENCE

Mindfulness doesn't just transform individual experiences, but its impact extends far beyond you. When I'm fully present in the moment, my children feel seen and valued, my team feels appreciated, and my sense of fulfillment improves. Presence creates a ripple effect by fostering an environment of trust, a collaborative mindset, and emotional connection.

Elon Musk's leadership illustrates this balance between intensity and presence. While his drive has led to groundbreaking innovation, his genuine engagement with his team has been credited with inspiring loyalty and creativity. These moments of presence remind us that even amid the busiest lives, small moments of connection hold immense power.

LESSONS LEARNED THE HARD WAY

Despite understanding the value of presence, the lure of distraction is relentless. I've learned that mindfulness is not just about achieving a perfect state but about relentlessly returning to the present again and again. It's about forgiving oneself for the moments you miss and recommitting to showing up fully in the moments ahead.

The hardest lesson is dealing with the time that's already passed: the events we missed, the laughter we weren't part of, and the stories we half-heard. But these moments also should fuel our determination to do better. They remind me that while I can't revisit the past, I can choose to write a different future, one deeply rooted in presence, connection, and love.

KEY THEMES:

1. **The Power of Presence:** Whether in relationships, work, or personal growth, being fully engaged is what makes the difference between a meaningful life and one that just passes by.
2. **Distraction Comes at a Cost:** The moments we miss—the ones where we're half-listening, half-scrolling, or lost in

thought—can never be recovered. There's wisdom in realizing what we've lost and using that awareness to change.
3. **Mindfulness Creates Fulfillment:** A mindful life isn't about perfection—it's about choosing to be present more often than not, allowing us to experience life with clarity and depth.

LESSONS AND REFLECTIONS:

1. **Recognizing the Impact of Distraction:** Think back to a time when you were physically present but mentally elsewhere. How did that affect the moment? What did you miss? How might things have been different if you had been fully engaged?
2. **Where Could Mindfulness Improve Your Life?** Look at your daily routines, your conversations, and your most important relationships. What areas would benefit from more focus, more attention, and fewer distractions?

ACTIONABLE STEPS:

1. **Commit to One Fully Present Activity Each Day:** Pick one thing—a meal, a conversation, a walk, or even just five minutes of silence. No phone, no multitasking. Just be there, fully engaged.
2. **Set an Intention to Minimize Distractions:** Each week, choose one area of your life where you will actively reduce distractions. Maybe it's putting your phone away during family time, turning off notifications during deep work, or setting boundaries around personal moments.
3. **Practice Gratitude for Small, Meaningful Moments:** At the end of each day, write down one moment where you truly felt present. Maybe it was a deep conversation, a moment of laughter, or just noticing the way the sun hit your window in the morning. The more you recognize these moments, the more they'll start to show up.

CONCLUSION:

The art of being present is not about removing distractions but about consciously choosing to engage with life. It's about recognizing that the most valuable gift we can give to ourselves, our loved ones, and the world is our attention.

As I continue this journey of life, I do so with the understanding that presence is both a practice and a gift. It transforms fleeting moments into lasting memories, infuses depth into relationships, and turns the ordinary into something extraordinary. By cultivating mindfulness, I am reminded that life's richness does not lie in what we achieve but in how deeply we experience each moment.

SIXTEEN
INTEGRATING THE JOURNEY
CREATING A LIFE OF HARMONY

Life isn't a smooth melody of harmony. Instead, it's more like a clash of chaos and fleeting moments of clarity. We are not really saints walking this earth with unwavering serenity; we are, in fact, humans, flawed and raw, swayed by emotions, actions, and the unpredictable nature of those around us.

Integration, in this context, does not mean we achieve a zen-like state that shields us from irritation, anger, or pain. It means interlacing the messiness of our human experience with moments of clarity, intention, and grace.

True harmony isn't about suppressing conflict or our natural emotions. It's about learning to live in the tension between peace and chaos, between what we aspire to be and who we truly are. In this chapter, we'll explore how to embrace these contradictions to create a life that is both practical and meaningful.

THE DUALITY OF HUMAN NATURE

Let's face it: inner peace is short-lived. You might spend the morning meditating, perfectly centered, only to find yourself cursing under your breath when someone cuts you off in traffic. You practice gratitude for your blessings, but when you see someone achieving something you've longed for, envy creeps in. This is the duality of human nature, the constant pull between our higher selves and our baser instincts.

I've been there: calm and composed in the boardroom, customer negotiations, and employee meetings, only to lose my temper over a trivial argument with a family member. I intentionally choose to be present with my children but often find my mind wandering to an unresolved issue at work. My inability to stay perfectly aligned with values infuriates me, but perhaps it's not about perfection at all; it may be about awareness. Integration begins when we stop pretending we are immune to these moments and instead learn to navigate them with honesty and humility.

THE DISRUPTIONS OF OTHERS

One of the greatest challenges to harmony is people. Let's not romanticize this: people can be very infuriating. A colleague undermines your hard work. A partner says something thoughtless. A friend withdraws without explanation. These moments sting because we are deeply interconnected, and the actions of others often disrupt our fragile sense of peace.

Take my professional life as an example. I've had employees who, despite their brilliance, lacked basic decency toward their peers. Their actions sowed discord, yet I relied on their expertise. In my personal life, I've struggled to stay patient with loved ones whose choices seemed reckless or hurtful. These situations create an internal battle: the desire to react with anger or judgment versus the aspiration to respond with compassion and understanding.

Let's be honest—sometimes, anger wins. Sometimes, we lash out or withdraw. And that's okay. Integration isn't about never getting carried away; it's about recognizing when we do and finding our way back.

EMBRACING THE MESSINESS

There's a myth that a harmonious life is one without conflict or chaos, where every decision aligns with our values and every interaction is smooth. That's a lie we tell ourselves to avoid facing the messiness of reality. Harmony isn't the absence of mess; it's the ability to embrace it.

Consider Rumi's profound statement, "The wound is the place where the light enters you." What if the chaos we relentlessly strive to avoid is actually the crucible of growth? Perhaps the most human moments—when we express our emotions, falter, or even cry—are the ones that offer us the most profound insights into our true selves.

For me, the most profound lessons have come from my failures to live up to my own standards. When I've snapped at my kids or made a thoughtless decision, the guilt that follows isn't just a punishment; it's a guide. It forces me to reflect, to ask how I can do better. It's in these moments of reckoning that I find the threads of integration, choosing to learn from the mess instead of running from it.

LIVING IN THE GRAY

If there's one truth I've learned, it's that life exists in the gray. We are not wholly good or bad, nor are the people around us. We make mistakes, hurt others, and let ourselves down. Yet, we also show kindness, strive for growth, and create beauty. Integration is about accepting this duality, both in ourselves and others.

When someone wrongs me, my initial reaction is rarely elegant. I've felt the sting of betrayal and the heat of resentment. But over time, I've come to see that holding onto these feelings only perpetuates the cycle of pain. Letting go doesn't mean condoning the hurt; it means refusing to let it define me. It's an act of reclaiming my energy and redirecting it toward what matters.

This doesn't happen overnight. Forgiveness and acceptance are not single moments but ongoing processes. They require effort, reflection, and the willingness to face our own imperfections. They require us to live in the gray, acknowledging that no one—not even ourselves—exists entirely on one side of the moral spectrum.

PRACTICAL HARMONY

So, how do we integrate these truths into our lives in a way that feels practical and real? Here's what I've found helpful:

1. **Own Your Reactions:** When someone's actions disrupt your peace, pause before responding. Acknowledge your emotions—anger, hurt, frustration—but don't let them dictate your actions. This pause creates a space where you can choose how to respond rather than react impulsively.

2. **Create Small Rituals**: Integration doesn't require grand gestures. It's in the small rituals—taking a deep breath before entering a meeting, setting aside five minutes to journal, or stepping outside for fresh air—that we create moments of harmony within the chaos.
3. **Learn from the Lows**: When you falter, don't rush to fix it. Sit with the discomfort, ask what it's teaching you, and use that insight to move forward. Every stumble is an opportunity to recalibrate.
4. **Balance Inner Peace with Outer Action:** Inner peace is important, but it's not a retreat from the world. It's the foundation that allows you to engage with life's messiness from a place of strength. Use it as a tool, not a hiding place.
5. **Forgive Yourself and Others:** Forgiveness is not a gift you give to others; it's a release you grant yourself. By letting go of resentment, you free yourself to move forward unburdened.

KEY THEMES:

1. **The Duality of Human Nature:** Acknowledge that we are both capable of great mindfulness and prone to being swept away by emotions and reactions.
2. **The Messiness of Reality:** Understand that harmony does not mean perfection or the absence of conflict but involves navigating and embracing life's chaos.
3. **Practical Integration:** Embrace the importance of small, consistent practices that integrate inner peace and external action in daily life.
4. **Living in the Gray:** Accept the complexity of human behavior, both in ourselves and others, as a natural part of the human experience.
5. **Growth Through Challenges:** Recognize failures and disruptions as opportunities to learn, recalibrate, and move forward with greater awareness.

LESSONS AND REFLECTIONS:

1. **Recognize the Interconnectedness of Life:** Every action, thought, and reaction ripples out to affect other areas of life, creating an interconnected web that requires attention and balance.
2. **Embrace Imperfection:** Life will always have moments of discord; the goal is not to eliminate them but to learn and grow from them.
3. **Value Forgiveness and Letting Go:** Releasing resentment toward ourselves and others frees us to create harmony in our interactions and decisions.
4. **Find Balance Between Inner and Outer Worlds:** True integration involves aligning the inner peace of mindfulness with the external realities of action and interaction.

ACTIONABLE STEPS:

1. **Pause and Reflect:** When faced with a triggering event or emotional reaction, pause and take three deep breaths. Use this pause to decide on a thoughtful, intentional response rather than reacting impulsively.
2. **Create Micro-Rituals:** Introduce small practices into your daily life that foster integration, such as journaling your thoughts for five minutes before bed or spending a mindful moment appreciating nature.
3. **Own Your Role in Conflict:** During conflicts with others, take a moment to reflect on how your actions or reactions might be contributing to the situation. Seek to respond from a place of understanding rather than defensiveness.
4. **Reframe Failures:** When setbacks occur, ask yourself what they are teaching you. Write down one lesson from the experience and one small action you can take to apply that lesson moving forward.
5. **Strengthen Emotional Resilience:** Use visualization exercises to prepare yourself for challenges. Imagine navigating a difficult situation with grace, focusing on how you want to feel and respond.

6. **Express Gratitude:** At the end of each day, list three things you are grateful for, focusing on experiences or interactions that have brought value to your life, no matter how small.
7. **Forgive and Move Forward:** Identify one person or situation you are holding resentment toward and make a conscious effort to release that negativity, whether through meditation, writing a letter (even if unsent), or speaking directly with them to resolve the issue.

CONCLUSION:

Integration isn't a finish line; it's a clash of contradictions, constantly shifting between struggle and clarity. It's about holding space for both the chaos and the calm, the saint and the sinner within us. It's about realizing that harmony doesn't mean the absence of conflict but the ability to dance with it.

As I continue this journey, I do so with the understanding that I will stumble, that I will falter, and that this is not a failure but part of the process. Harmony isn't found in perfection; it's found in the raw, gritty, emotional mess of being human. It's found in the moments when we choose, despite our flaws and frustrations, to move forward with intention, humility, and grace.

In those moments, perhaps, we glimpse the truest essence of what it means to live a life of integration.

SEVENTEEN
EMBRACING UNCERTAINTY
TRUSTING THE UNKNOWN

Uncertainty is a terrible beast that waits in the shadows of our lives. It doesn't knock or ask for permission. It just barges in, turning your well-scripted plans into fine rubble. It is terrifying and deeply maddening, yet strangely liberating. I have spent years trying to outwit uncertainty, wrestling it into submission with plans, contingency strategies, and spreadsheets. But the truth is, uncertainty doesn't give a damn about your intelligence. It laughs in the face of control and does its thing.

Yet, amidst uncertainty's chaos lies potential—potential for growth, for creativity, for something completely unexpected. But let's not sugarcoat it. Embracing uncertainty isn't some enlightened walk in the park. It is, in fact, a gut-wrenching confrontation with your fears, insecurities, and the very fabric of what you think you know about life.

THE RAW HUMAN CONDITION: WRESTLING WITH THE UNKNOWN

Here's the thing about uncertainty: it feeds on our need for control. We plan, strategize, and build routines to insulate ourselves from the unpredictable. But life doesn't play by those rules. I've experienced this firsthand: the fear of losing something irreplaceable, the anxiety of waiting for news that could shatter your plans, and the silent, creeping dread of not knowing what comes next.

It's natural to resist. We're human. No amount of mindfulness or self-help books will erase the fact that we are deeply affected by what happens around us. Jiddu Krishnamurti's concept of freedom from the known is profound, but let's not pretend it's easy. Letting go of the known feels like stepping into the void without a safety net. The mind rebels, clinging to fragments of certainty like a drowning man grasping for air.

And then there's Rumi, the eternal romantic, whispering, "Try not to resist the changes that come your way." Easier said than done, Rumi. When uncertainty barges in, it's not poetry—it's sleepless nights, explosive arguments, and a thousand "what ifs" eating away at your peace. Yet, even in its most brutal form, uncertainty is where transformation begins. The struggle itself is where the magic happens.

TRUSTING IN THE PROCESS: A BRUTAL ACT OF FAITH

Trust is such a fragile thing. We often talk about trusting the process and trusting life, but in the midst of the chaos of uncertainty, trust feels like an ultimate gamble. It's stepping forward without a guarantee, leaping into the unknown with only a whisper of hope. Trust means risking failure, heartbreak, and deep disappointment. Yet, without trust, we stagnate. Growth becomes impossible, and we're left with the suffocating weight of what might have been.

I've wrestled with this myself every day. Trusting in uncertainty is grounded courage but not blind faith. It's about looking uncertainty in the eye and saying, "I really don't know what's coming, but I'll meet it anyway." It's about understanding that uncertainty isn't a void; it's a canvas waiting for your next move.

RELATIONSHIPS: WHERE UNCERTAINTY REIGNS SUPREME

Uncertainty is never more brutal than in relationships. People are unpredictable, inconsistent, and maddeningly human. And as you age, the stakes grow higher. When you're young, finding friends or falling in love feels effortless, unburdened by the weight of past experiences, and your mind is filled with hope. But as the years add up, so does the baggage. The gamble deepens. Façades unravel with brutal honesty. Relationships fizzle before they even blossom, weighed down by mistrust and the scars of disappointment.

I've felt this sting—the collapse of relationships I once believed unshakable, the duality of human connections that unravel in ways I couldn't predict. Partners grow in unexpected directions. Friends drift, and even your children, your own flesh and blood, transform before your eyes into strangers navigating their own uncertainties. But here's what I've learned: relationships are mirrors. They reflect not just beauty but chaos. They expose your fears, insecurities, and capacity for both connection and destruction.

Embracing uncertainty in relationships means letting go of guarantees and perfection that you long for. It's about being present, vulnerable, and willing to adapt. It's messy, heartbreaking even, but it's also where the deepest connections are forged.

THE CULT OF CERTAINTY

And what about those who promise certainty? The gurus, the cult leaders, the so-called saints who claim to have answers? They sell certainty to the broken-hearted and the desperate—packaged as salvation, enlightenment, or life engineering.

Think of modern Swamijis and their sprawling empire of ashrams and volunteers. Their promise of transformation or "Inner Engineering" lures people seeking meaning in the chaos of existence But ask yourself: Do they emerge transformed? Or are they just caught in a new cycle of dependency, trading one illusion for another?

It's not just spiritual leaders. Think of the scandals that plague the Vatican, the pastors caught in cycles of abuse, and the so-called representatives of God who exploit trust for personal gain. Contrast this with saints like Swami Vivekananda, who never sought to control or manipulate. He inspired through selflessness, leaving people stronger, not tethered. Modern cults of personality thrive on uncertainty, selling it back to the masses as clarity while building empires on the fragility of hope.

PRACTICAL STEPS FOR LIVING WITH UNCERTAINTY

Living with uncertainty is messy, imperfect, and deeply human. Here's how I've learned to navigate it:

1. **Reframe the Unknown:** Instead of asking, "What if it goes wrong?" ask, "What if this is the start of something better?"
2. **Anchor Yourself in the Present:** Practice mindfulness to ground yourself in the here and now, pulling yourself out of the spiral of "what ifs."
3. **Set Intentions, Not Expectations:** Focus on how you approach uncertainty—calmly, curiously, and with courage—rather than clinging to outcomes.
4. **Lean on Your People:** Share your fears, seek advice, and let others remind you of your strength.
5. **Take Small, Brave Steps:** Fear loses its power when you take action, no matter how small.
6. **Reflect on Past Resilience:** Let your history of surviving the unknown remind you of your strength.

KEY THEMES:

1. **The Fear of Uncertainty:** Fear is universal yet deeply personal, challenging us to grow.
2. **Trusting the Process:** Trust isn't the absence of fear; it's choosing courage despite it.
3. **Relationships and Unpredictability:** Embrace the duality of connection—its beauty and its chaos.
4. **The Gift of Uncertainty:** Learn to see the unknown as a source of creativity, growth, and possibility.

LESSONS AND REFLECTIONS:

1. **You're Not Supposed to Have All the Answers:** Nobody has life completely figured out. What is the difference between those who move forward and those who stay stuck? They take action anyway. Waiting until you feel "ready" is just another way of standing still.
2. **Fear and Excitement Feel the Same:** Your heart races, your breath quickens, your mind speeds up. Is it fear, or is it anticipation? The only real difference is the meaning you attach to it. What if you stopped labeling it as fear and started calling it possibility?

3. **Control is an Illusion:** No matter how much you plan, life will always have its own ideas. You can fight it, or you can learn to flow with it. The sooner you stop trying to control everything, the more at peace you'll be—and the more open you'll become to opportunities you never expected.

ACTIONABLE STEPS:

1. **Pause and Reframe:** When uncertainty arises, ask how it might lead to unexpected opportunities.
2. **Practice Letting Go:** Release one thing you're clinging to and allow life to flow without control.
3. **Find Your Anchor:** Develop a grounding ritual to center yourself during chaos.

CONCLUSION:

Uncertainty is not a problem to be solved. It's a paradox to be lived. It's the tension between fear and hope, chaos and creativity, loss and possibility. It's not pretty, and it's certainly not easy. But it's also where life happens, in the unscripted, unpredictable spaces where we're forced to let go of control and simply be. We're not saints, and we're not supposed to be. We're human: beautifully flawed, endlessly curious, and maddeningly complex.

Embracing uncertainty doesn't mean loving it. It means respecting it, learning from it, and allowing it to shape us in ways we never could have imagined. So, here's my challenge to you: Stop waiting for certainty. Start living in the mess. It's terrifying, yes, but it's also where the magic happens.

EIGHTEEN
NAVIGATING SUCCESS AND FAILURE
REDEFINING ACHIEVEMENT

Success and failure are human constructs, fragile markers we cling to in an attempt to give life meaning, a dose to our ego, and a reason to compare and, in many cases, put down people around us. Society celebrates success with applause and accolades while treating failure as a scar to be hidden, a shame.

In reality, success and failure are inseparable twins. They are intertwined like shadows and light and celebrated like day and night. Neither exists without the other, and both are fleeting. Success may fill your lungs with pride, but failure may strip you bare, leaving you gasping for clarity and a lifeline.

For years, I chased success relentlessly. I imagined it was a straight road paved with milestones, and with hard work and intelligence, it could be achieved in bigger and better ways. I built businesses, chased financial glory, and grabbed at the external markers that shouted, "You've made it!"

But the hollowness that followed every win whispered a deeper truth—success is not an endpoint. It's an evolution, a euphoric state, a fleeting high that forces you to keep climbing. And failure? Failure is not the end; it's the spark that reignites the fire when the embers grow cold.

STANDING TALL AMIDST THE STORM

In one of my ventures, I stood tall for years, refusing to bow to the pressure of slow growth. Success was elusive, flirting with me just enough to keep me going. When it finally arrived, it wasn't a triumphant roar but a measured high. Though fulfilling, it left me feeling incomplete. The business had achieved what it was meant to, bringing value and glory, but not the financial windfall I had envisioned. Then came the question that haunts every creator: "Should I stay and push for more, or is it time to let go?"

Walking away wasn't easy. The temptation to keep riding the wave is real. Giving up a golden goose that has started laying the eggs isn't easy. But deep down, I knew that clinging to comfort breeds stagnation and, ultimately, runs your life. Lifestyle, purpose, and the call to create something bigger pulled me in another direction. I moved on, not because I had failed or reached eternal glory, but because the journey demanded it. Sometimes, knowing when to leave is the hardest and most courageous choice.

THE ILLUSION OF SUCCESS AND THE BRUTALITY OF FAILURE

Success is often romanticized as a glittering trophy displayed to validate one's worth. But what is success, really? A fleeting moment, a fragile construct to satisfy our egos momentarily. Success can blind you and seduce you into thinking you've reached the summit. In reality, all you've done is scale one mountain in a range of endless peaks.

Failure, however, doesn't lie. It's raw, unfiltered, and brutally honest. It strips away pretenses, forcing you to confront your deepest fears and insecurities. My first monumental failure, the dissolution of my marriage, was not just personal; it was truly existential. With great fanfare, I had married a person, a family, a dream. And when it fell apart, it felt like my identity had crumbled, and I'd lost my carefully crafted world. The ripple effect touched everything: my four children, my work, my sense of self.

For years, I tormented myself with questions. Where did I go wrong? Could I have done more? Was this failure mine to own, or was it simply destiny at play? The answers never came neatly packaged. But what I learned is that failure is not your enemy. It's a ruthless teacher that strips to your core. It revealed the deepest parts of me that needed healing, the priorities I had ignored, and the strength I never knew I had.

LEARNING FROM GIANTS WHO WALKED THROUGH FIRE

History is filled with stories of those who found greatness through repeated failures. These are not fairy tales but raw, gritty accounts of human resilience:

1. **Colonel Harland Sanders** pitched his chicken recipe over a thousand times before creating the empire known as KFC. He started in his 60s, proving that persistence doesn't recognize age.
2. **J. K. Rowling** battled rejection after rejection before Harry Potter became a global phenomenon. At her lowest, she was a single mother on welfare, living with depression. Her belief in her story carried her through.
3. **Steve Jobs**, fired from Apple—the very company he co-founded—turned his exile into an opportunity. He built Pixar and NeXT, redefining industries, and returned to Apple with a vision that transformed it into a global powerhouse.

These stories resonate because they echo our own struggles. Success and failure are never final. They are stepping stones, with each one contributing to the masterpiece of our lives.

THE COST OF STAYING TOO LONG

The hardest lesson I've learned is knowing when to leave. Whether it's a failing relationship, a stagnating venture, or a dream that no longer serves its purpose, staying too long can poison what you've built and seep into the areas that are strong, weakening and eventually destroying them. We cling because we're afraid of what letting go might mean. But the truth is, leaving isn't failure; it's courage.

Think of Napoleon Bonaparte, a man who built an empire through sheer force of will, only to lose it all when he couldn't recognize when to stop. His relentless ambition led him to power, but his inability to step back led to exile—twice. Contrast that with George Washington, who willingly stepped away after two terms, refusing to let power consume him. They understood what many leaders fail to grasp: knowing when to walk away is just as important as knowing when to fight.

TURNING PAIN INTO PURPOSE

Pain is an inevitable part of life, and every human is bound to experience it, but suffering is a choice. The pain of failure doesn't disappear—it lingers, reshaping you in ways you can't always see. But if you let it, pain can fuel your purpose. It can deepen your empathy, sharpen your focus, and clarify what truly matters in life.

The pain of my marriage dissolving forced me to confront the parts of myself I had long ignored. It made me a better father, a more empathetic leader, and a man unafraid to face his flaws. The professional setbacks? They became the forge where my resilience was tempered. Every failure taught me to value the process over the outcome, the journey over the destination.

KEY THEMES:

1. **Success and Failure as Partners:** They are not opposites but essential elements of growth.
2. **Knowing When to Move On:** Recognize when it's time to leave, not in defeat but as evolution.
3. **The Slow Path to Growth:** Success is a journey, not a destination.
4. **Redefining Metrics:** True achievement is about purpose, alignment, and resilience.

LESSONS AND REFLECTIONS:

1. **Success is Personal:** If you don't define success for yourself, someone else will do it for you—and chances are, it won't align with what truly makes you happy. Don't spend your life chasing a dream that wasn't even yours to begin with.
2. **Failure is the Best Feedback You'll Ever Get:** Every setback, every wrong turn, every idea that flops—it's all just data. It's the universe telling you what doesn't work so you can get closer to what does. The only real failure? Giving up before you figure it out.
3. **Money and Titles Don't Mean Fulfillment:** There are plenty of people with all the money, status, and recognition in

the world who still feel empty. So what actually makes you feel alive? What excites you, challenges you, and gives your life meaning? That's the real measure of success.

ACTIONABLE STEPS FOR NAVIGATING SUCCESS AND FAILURE

1. **Redefine Success:** Let go of society's metrics. Define success on your terms—alignment with your values, the impact you create, and the person you become.
2. **Reframe Failure:** List your failures and identify the lessons they taught you. Celebrate the growth they triggered.
3. **Set Intentions, Not Goals:** Goals can be rigid; intentions are adaptable. Focus on how you want to live, not just on what you want to achieve.
4. **Learn When to Leave:** Evaluate what no longer serves you. Walk away when staying costs more than it gives.
5. **Embrace the Slow Burn:** Growth takes time. Commit to the process, even when progress feels invisible.

CONCLUSION:

You think failure is the end until you realize you have to wake up the next day and keep going anyway. You think success is the peak until you find yourself asking, 'Now what?' Neither stays. You just keep moving, Money and titles don't mean fulfillment. They are the very rhythm of life, the highs and lows that create the music of your existence. Failure will humble you. Success will uplift you. Together, they will shape you into someone you never imagined you could be.

Keep going. Keep learning. Keep creating. And remember, the greatest success isn't measured by titles or wealth; it's in the courage to keep becoming, even when the path is uncertain.

NINETEEN
THE BALANCE OF SOLITUDE AND CONNECTION
FINDING HARMONY IN RELATIONSHIPS

When my first big failure struck, it felt like the ground beneath me had given way. My instincts immediately pushed me into isolation to seek solace in the quiet corners of my existence. I seethed in anger at disappointing so many people around me.

For someone who lived, thrived, and aspired to create an environment of laughter and camaraderie, this retreat was a big departure from my natural habitat. Yet, there was peace in that seclusion—a stillness that allowed me to run through the worst of my emotions, reflect, and, eventually, rebuild.

This chapter explores the delicate dance between solitude and connection, the forces that shape our relationships, and the roadmap to achieving harmony between the two to bring out the best of yourself. For me, and perhaps for many, it was in the space between solitude and connection that I discovered a new way of being.

THE HEALING POWER OF SOLITUDE

Solitude, though often confused with loneliness, became my sanctuary. It was not the absence of people but the presence of myself. In those quiet moments, I found the clarity that had evaded me during the noise of success and failure. Solitude became the space where I could process my emotions, confront my shortcomings, and ask the difficult questions that life demanded of me.

Albert Einstein famously credited solitude for his creative breakthroughs. His long walks and quiet contemplation were where he envisioned the theories that completely reshaped our understanding of the universe. Solitude, for Einstein, was not isolation but incubation; it was a fertile ground for new ideas and perspectives.

In my solitude, I began to dismantle the walls I had let the shame of failure build around me. I confronted the guilt of my marriage's dissolution, the regret of missed moments with my children, and the fear of vulnerability. It was in these moments of raw introspection that I began to rebuild—not a life of perfection, but one of authenticity.

THE NECESSITY OF CONNECTION

Solitude alone is not enough, and as humans, we are wired for connection. Relationships are where we test our growth, where we translate inner transformation into outer impact. The challenge lies in balancing the need for self-reflection with the vulnerability required to engage with others.

Viktor Frankl, Holocaust survivor and author of *Man's Search for Meaning*, found a profound connection even in the depths of unimaginable suffering. He wrote that meaning often arises through relationships, whether in the love we give, the sacrifices we make, or the compassion we show. His story reminds us that even in solitude, connection can be a beacon of hope.

For me, rebuilding connections meant stepping out of my self-imposed isolation and comfort zone. It required courage to show up for my children, to face their questions and their pain. It demanded vulnerability to reconnect with friends and colleagues, even under the fear of judgment. Eventually, I learned that the strength I had cultivated in solitude could be the foundation for deeper and more authentic relationships.

THE PUSH AND PULL OF BALANCE

The balance between solitude and connection is not static. Life's demands, emotions, and circumstances constantly shift the scales. There were times when I leaned too heavily on solitude, using it as a shield to avoid the messiness of human relationships. Other times, I immersed myself in connection, losing touch with the quiet voice within me that needed space to breathe.

Maya Angelou balanced a life of public connection with the sanctity of private reflection. Her poetry and activism were deeply informed by her ability to retreat into herself, to find strength and inspiration in solitude. Angelou's life is a testament to the power of balancing the inner and outer worlds.

In my own journey, I found that balance required intentionality. Solitude and connection are not opposing forces but complementary energies. Solitude fuels connection by grounding us in our truth. Connection enriches solitude by giving us stories, experiences, and love to reflect on.

LESSONS FROM SOLITUDE AND CONNECTION

1. **Solitude as a Mirror:** Solitude reveals who we truly are without the noise of others' expectations. It's a place to confront our fears, celebrate our growth, and recalibrate our lives.
2. **Connection as a Catalyst:** Relationships challenge us to grow. They demand empathy, patience, and courage, pushing us to become more compassionate and resilient.
3. **The Interplay:** Solitude without connection risks isolation. Connection without solitude risks burnout. The balance lies in honoring both needs and allowing them to feed into each other.

REBUILDING RELATIONSHIPS: A ROAD MAP

1. **Start Small:** After a period of isolation, re-entering relationships can feel daunting. Begin with small, intentional acts of connection—a call to a friend, a shared meal with family, or a simple expression of gratitude.
2. **Practice Presence:** Whether in solitude or connection, be fully present. In solitude, sit with your thoughts without distraction. In connection, listen deeply, free from judgment or interruption.
3. **Set Boundaries:** Balance requires boundaries. Protect your

solitude by carving out time for reflection. Honor your connections by showing up fully when you engage with others.
4. **Seek Meaningful Relationships:** Not all connections are equal. Prioritize relationships that nourish and challenge you, those built on mutual respect and authenticity.
5. **Reflect and Adjust:** Regularly evaluate your balance. Are you retreating too much into solitude? Are you losing yourself in the demands of others? Adjust as needed to maintain harmony.

KEY THEMES:

1. **The Duality of Human Needs:** Solitude and connection are not opposites but essential, interdependent forces.
2. **Rebuilding After Failure:** Solitude provides the foundation for self-discovery, while connection offers the opportunity for renewal.
3. **Finding Balance:** Harmony comes from intentionality—choosing when to step back and when to lean in.

LESSONS AND REFLECTIONS:

1. **You Need Both Solitude and Connection:** Too much isolation, and you feel disconnected from the world. Too much dependence on others, and you lose yourself. The key isn't choosing one or the other—it's learning to balance both.
2. **Being Alone and Being Lonely Aren't the Same Thing:** There's a difference between choosing solitude and feeling abandoned. One empowers you, the other drains you. The challenge is recognizing when you need space and when you need support.
3. **Quality Over Quantity in Relationships:** You don't need a hundred people in your life—you need the right ones. The ones who challenge you, support you, and make you better. The depth of your connections matters more than the number of them.
4. **Your Relationship with Yourself Sets the Tone for Every Other Relationship:** If you don't know who you are when you're alone, you'll struggle to show up fully in any connection.

Learning to be comfortable in your own company makes every other relationship stronger.

ACTIONABLE STEPS:

1. **Schedule Solitude:** Dedicate 30 minutes daily to quiet reflection, journaling, or meditation. Use this time to reconnect with yourself.
2. **Prioritize Quality Over Quantity:** Focus on forging deep, meaningful connections rather than spreading yourself too thin across superficial interactions.
3. **Balance Emotional Energy:** Monitor your emotional state. If you're feeling drained, lean into solitude. If you're feeling isolated, reach out to someone you trust.
4. **Create Rituals:** Establish rituals that honor both solitude and connection—like a solo morning walk followed by a family dinner.
5. **Practice Gratitude:** Whether in solitude or connection, reflect on what you're grateful for. Gratitude bridges the gap between the inner and outer worlds.

CONCLUSION:

The balance between solitude and connection is not a destination but a well-choreographed dance, one that requires constant adjustment, awareness, and grace. Solitude teaches us who we are; connection shows us who we can become. Together, they form the foundation of a life that is both grounded and expansive.

As I continue this journey, I do so with the understanding that failure, solitude, and connection are not separate chapters but threads in the same story woven to form the true "me." They have taught me that rebuilding a life of harmony is not about choosing one over the other but about honoring both, finding strength in the stillness, and joy in the embrace of others.

TWENTY
EMPATHY AND LEADERSHIP
CREATING IMPACT THROUGH COMPASSION

For most of my life, my approach to leadership has been deeply personal, raw, and often chaotic. It was forged in the crucible of ambition and loyalty, driven by relationships that spanned decades. Many of those who worked alongside me weren't just employees—they were friends, confidants, and comrades in arms, people I trusted to walk through fire with me. However, trust and loyalty, while invaluable, bring their own storms that you need to deal with.

This chapter is about navigating those storms. It's about leading not just with strategy but with heart—about finding the balance between ambition and compassion, control and connection. Leadership, I've come to understand, isn't just about inspiring others to reach goals; it's about standing beside them in their struggles and celebrating their triumphs as if they were your own.

THE EVOLUTION OF MY LEADERSHIP

For years, my leadership style was unapologetically direct. I built a team of trusted soldiers—people who could be counted on to deliver no matter the odds. We succeeded because we intimately knew each other's strengths, weaknesses, and quirks. Many had been with me for over two decades, and together, we built organizations, products, and systems that pushed boundaries. Yet, that closeness also bred challenges. Conflict management in a tight-knit team is like navigating a minefield—you know where the mines are, but one wrong step can still blow everything apart.

Adding new voices to such an ecosystem was always a gamble. When senior hires entered our world, their expertise often clashed with the familial bonds we'd built. I learned that leadership meant bridging those gaps, integrating differing styles, and ensuring that the mission remained greater than individual egos.

Failures were my harshest teachers. When my first marriage crumbled, leaving behind shattered dreams and four children navigating the aftermath, I couldn't escape the parallels between my personal and professional life. Just as I had often let conflicts fester within my teams, I had ignored the emotional cracks in my personal relationships. That failure was a wake-up call—a reminder that leadership isn't just about driving forward but about nurturing the people who walk beside you.

EMPATHY IN LEADERSHIP: THE TURNING POINT

Empathy isn't a soft skill; it's a courageous one. It requires leaders to wade into the discomfort of vulnerability, feel the weight of another's struggle, and acknowledge their own. I learned that moments of true connection came not from issuing directives but from listening, truly listening with no agenda other than simply to understand.

Howard Schultz, former CEO of Starbucks, who built his empire on a foundation of empathy, is a great example of empathetic leadership. After witnessing his father's struggles with unemployment, Schultz vowed to create a company culture that treated employees as partners, offering benefits like health care and stock options even to part-time workers. Schultz's leadership did not just revolve around scaling a business; instead, it was about honoring humanity within it.

Leading a team through challenging economic shifts taught me the importance of empathy as a stabilizer. When layoffs loomed, I chose transparency, sitting with my team and laying out the circumstances openly. I didn't have all the answers, but I had an open heart and a willingness to share the burden. Those conversations were hard, but they forged a trust that carried us through the storm.

THE DOUBLE-EDGED SWORD OF EMPATHY

Empathy is highly transformative but comes with its own challenges. There were times when I allowed myself to absorb too much of others' pain, mistaking leadership for martyrdom. Empathy isn't about solving everyone's problems or carrying their weight; it's about walking beside them while empowering them to carry their own.

Jacinda Ardern, New Zealand's former prime minister, is another great example of empathetic leadership, as, during the Christchurch mosque shootings, she inspired the world. Her response was swift, compassionate, and deeply human. Most importantly, she balanced this empathy with decisive action. Ardern's example underscores a point of view that empathy in leadership is not about being soft but about being strong enough to act from a place of understanding.

In my case, I had to learn boundaries. Leading empathetically doesn't mean neglecting your well-being. It means cultivating the strength to support others while staying grounded in your clarity and purpose.

PERSONAL TRANSFORMATION – EMPATHY IN RELATIONSHIPS

Empathy didn't just reshape my professional life; it transformed my personal relationships. Empathy became my bridge to understanding my children's unique worlds. Instead of imposing my perspective, I began to ask questions, to sit with their frustrations, and to meet them where they were. This wasn't easy, requiring a complete shift in how I dealt with my first child vs. my fourth child. There were moments of raw guilt—realizing how often I'd been physically present but emotionally absent.

In my romantic relationships, empathy became a cornerstone of trust. Vulnerability, I learned, is the language of love, and empathy is its translator. It's not about fixing the other person but about holding space for their fears and dreams, even when they clash with your own. It's about the courage to say, "I don't fully understand, but I'm here to try."

A CULTURE OF EMPATHY IN LEADERSHIP

Leadership isn't just about individual transformation; it's about creating a culture where empathy thrives and transformation happens with people. It means fostering psychological safety, a space where people feel valued, heard, and free to take risks. It also means recognizing that behind every job title is a human being with a story, struggle, and dream.

Building a culture of empathetic leadership requires some deep intention. I've seen how simple acts of acknowledging a team member's hard work, offering flexibility for personal challenges, or even just asking, "How are you really doing?" can ripple outward. This often creates an environment of trust and collaboration. Empathy, when embedded in leadership, becomes a multiplier of morale and innovation.

LESSONS FROM FAMOUS FAILURES AND SUCCESSES

The world is replete with stories of leaders who rebuilt themselves and their organizations through empathy. Think of Oprah Winfrey, whose journey from a traumatic childhood to one of the most influential media figures was driven by her ability to connect deeply with people's stories. Or Steve Jobs, whose early years as a volatile leader gave way to a more empathetic approach when he returned to Apple, inspiring his team to create some of the most iconic products of our time.

These examples remind us that leadership is not static—it evolves as we do. Empathy is not a fixed trait but a skill we can cultivate, a lens through which we can reframe every interaction.

KEY THEMES:

1. **The Shift from Control to Connection**: Leadership is not about dictating but about understanding and empowering.
2. **Empathy as a Strength, Not a Weakness:** Empathy fuels trust, innovation, and resilience.
3. **Balancing Vulnerability with Strength:** Leadership demands both compassion and decisive action.

LESSONS AND REFLECTIONS:

1. **People Follow Leaders Who Care:** You can have **power, money, and influence**, but if the people around you don't feel

2. **Being Nice and Being a Leader Aren't the Same Thing:** You can be kind without being a pushover. Strong leadership isn't about avoiding conflict or making everyone happy—it's about knowing when to stand firm, when to compromise, and when to listen.
  3. **Real Leadership Leaves a Legacy:** The impact of a leader isn't measured by how many people worked under them—but by how many people grew because of them. A true leader creates opportunities, builds confidence in others, and leaves behind something greater than themselves.

ACTIONABLE STEPS FOR EMPATHETIC LEADERSHIP:

1. **Active Listening:** Practice listening without interruption or judgment. Focus fully on the speaker and reflect what you hear.
2. **Create Psychological Safety:** Foster an environment where people feel safe to share their ideas, concerns, and emotions without fear of judgment.
3. **Lead with Vulnerability:** Share your challenges and mistakes. Vulnerability creates connection and builds trust.
4. **Check In Regularly:** Whether in professional or personal settings, ask people how they're doing—not just superficially but genuinely.
5. **Set Healthy Boundaries:** Balance empathy with self-care. Recognize that you can support others without carrying their burdens.

CONCLUSION:

Empathy is not an accessory to leadership; it is its heart. When applied with intention, it transforms transactions into relationships, directives into dialogues, and workplaces into communities. As I continue this journey, I carry with me the understanding that leadership is not about perfection but about presence. It's about showing up fully with intention, listening deeply, and acting with integrity.

Through empathy, we don't just lead; we create impact. We build bridges where there were walls, find solutions where there were impasses, and inspire trust where there was doubt. In doing so, we not only transform others—we transform ourselves.

TWENTY-ONE
THE JOURNEY CONTINUES
EMBRACING LIFELONG GROWTH

As I continue to reflect on the path I have walked, one truth echoes very clearly: the journey of growth never ends. Each revelation, each misstep, and each breakthrough has been part of a deeper unfolding, a reminder that growth is not a destination but a way of living. It is humbling and exhilarating to realize that life's lessons are inexhaustible and the work of becoming is infinite.

GROWTH AS A NONLINEAR PATH

In my earlier years, I mistakenly believed growth followed a neat trajectory, that one success would build seamlessly upon another, and I was very much in control of the process. But life, as it often does, taught me otherwise. Growth is unpredictably messy, cyclical, and often bewildering. For every step forward, there were times I stumbled backward, entangled in fear, ego, or doubt.

There were many moments when failure loomed so large that it eclipsed everything else. My first marriage was a cataclysmic failure in my eyes, something that pushed me into corners of shame and regret. For years, I questioned what went wrong, spiraling into self-recrimination. But as time passed, I saw that failure is not a full stop; it is a comma, a pause in life's journey to reassess and rewrite the story. I learned to find grace in my missteps, to see them not as failures but as invitations to grow.

Consider Nelson Mandela, who, after 27 years of imprisonment, emerged not bitter or broken but renewed, embodying forgiveness and resilience. Mandela's story is a significant testament that growth often emerges from the ashes of pain and despair. It reminds us that even our darkest chapters are not the end but fertile ground for transformation.

THE COMMITMENT TO LIFELONG LEARNING

To grow is to remain open to new ideas and perspectives and even to the possibility of being wrong. It is an act of courage to look inward, face the parts of ourselves that resist change, and choose growth over comfort.

In my professional life, this commitment manifested in ways that I didn't expect. Early ventures taught me the price of rushing success, of pushing for outcomes without allowing processes to unfold naturally. Some businesses didn't yield the financial windfalls I envisioned, but they taught me lessons that became the foundation for future successes.

I think of Colonel Harland Sanders, who faced rejection over a thousand times before his fried chicken recipe gained traction. At 65, when most would consider giving up, he leaned into his failures and turned them into triumphs. While I absolutely despise eating KFC, his story still reminds me that growth demands persistence, and it's never too late to start fresh.

BALANCING PROGRESS AND PATIENCE

Growth isn't about relentless striving; it's about finding the rhythm between effort and surrender. There were periods in my life when I believed that relentless action was the only path forward. But this mindset often led to burnout and disconnection. Now I strive to balance progress with patience. I've learned to honor the seasons of life—moments of intense creation balanced by moments of quiet reflection. Growth, I've realized, doesn't always look like forward momentum. Sometimes, it looks like rest, stillness, or even letting go.

LESSONS FROM SOLITUDE AND CONNECTION

Growth is both an internal and external process. Solitude has been my sanctuary, a place where I have confronted my deepest fears and rediscovered my strength. But solitude alone is not enough; growth also requires connection.

Rebuilding relationships with my children after my divorce was not easy, but it was essential. Shedding resentment and anger wasn't easy, but I realized I needed to do it so I could have the strength to create a stable parenting and also not disappoint the work family that trusted me to create something magical. I had to step outside of my guilt and pride and meet them where they were with humility and love.

More often than not, when you are in a position of power, your instability radiates into everyone around you, and you are unknowingly putting them through a similar emotional journey, one they don't deserve. These moments of connection reminded me that growth is not just about self-improvement but about creating spaces where others can thrive alongside you.

EMBRACING THE UNFINISHED JOURNEY

One of the hardest truths to accept is that we are always unfinished. The ego craves completion, a sense of having arrived, but the soul knows that life is an eternal becoming. I've come to see that the work of self-discovery, healing, and growth is never done—and that's the beauty of it.

Take J. K. Rowling, who faced rejection after rejection before Harry Potter became a phenomenon. Her journey wasn't linear; it was marked by hardship and perseverance. Even after achieving monumental success, she continues to evolve, using her platform to explore new creative and philanthropic ventures. Her story reminds me that growth isn't confined to any single chapter of life—it continues as long as we do.

KEY THEMES:

1. **Growth as a Lifelong Process:** Understand that growth is not a linear journey but an ongoing process of becoming.
2. **The Role of Failure in Transformation:** Failure is not the end but a catalyst for deeper learning and growth.
3. **Balancing Action and Reflection:** Progress requires both effort and the patience to let things unfold.

LESSONS AND REFLECTIONS:

1. **You Never "Arrive":** There's no magical point where everything makes sense, and you've got it all figured out. Growth isn't a destination—it's a lifelong process of learning, adapting, and evolving.
2. **Stay Curious:** The moment you think you've mastered it all, you stop growing. The most successful and fulfilled people? They stay open, they keep questioning, and they never lose their hunger to learn.
3. **Every Chapter is Part of the Story:** Even the hard parts. Even the messy parts. Especially the messy parts. They shape you, challenge you, and prepare you for what's next. The story isn't just in the victories—it's in how you handle the setbacks, too.

ACTIONABLE STEPS FOR LIFELONG GROWTH:

1. **Reflect Daily:** Set aside time each evening to reflect on what you've learned, what challenged you, and how you responded to life's events.
2. **Embrace Failure as Feedback:** Instead of fearing failure, analyze it. What did it teach you? How can it shape your next steps?
3. **Stay Open to Change:** Be willing to adapt your perspectives and actions as new information and experiences arise.
4. **Balance Solitude and Connection:** Make time for self-reflection, but also seek meaningful connections that challenge and inspire you.
5. **Set Small, Evolving Goals:** Focus on incremental growth rather than overwhelming changes. Adjust your goals as you grow.

CONCLUSION:

As I move forward, I carry with me the understanding that life is not about arriving at a perfect version of myself but about embracing the process of becoming. Growth is not a straight line; it's a dance between progress and setbacks, certainty and doubt, solitude and connection.

The journey continues—not because I haven't grown enough but because there is always more to discover, more to create, and more to give. I step into each day with curiosity and courage, knowing that the work of becoming is the most meaningful work of all.

TWENTY-TWO
A LIFE OF PURPOSE AND PRESENCE

This journey has been anything but easy. It has been raw, unfiltered, and deeply human. I have faced the highs and lows of life, moments of rise followed by disappointing setbacks, only to find myself rising again. It's nothing but a reflection of the sheer grit and adaptability of the human spirit, a stark reminder that we are all capable of far more than we imagine.

For years, I measured success by what others could see: the applause, the accolades, the financial milestones. Yet, it was in the quiet moments of failure and honest reflection that I stumbled upon a more profound understanding. True fulfillment doesn't come from chasing perfection but from learning to be fully present in the life we have right now.

A BRUTAL TRUTH: THERE IS NO DESTINATION

For decades, I clung to the belief that there was an arrival point—a moment when life would finally make sense, when I would feel whole, unshaken, and complete. This was the lie I told myself to justify the sacrifices, sleepless nights, and neglected relationships.

But the truth? There is no final destination. The moment we reach the peak of one mountain, another one emerges. This realization is not a defeat but a liberation. Life doesn't owe us a neat, packaged ending tied up in a bow. It owes us nothing but the raw, unfiltered experience of being alive, filled with heartbreaks, joys, doubt, and discovery. And within that chaotic, imperfect journey lies its brilliance: the brilliance of waking up every day and trying again.

PRESENCE OVER PERFECTION

The relentless pursuit of perfection is a thief. It robs you of the now, of the raw, unfiltered beauty of simply existing. My failures have been my most ruthless teachers. They stripped me of my illusions, forced me into corners I didn't want to face, and showed me the cost of chasing the wrong things.

I remember moments of hollow success—standing on stage, receiving applause from strangers while feeling like a stranger to my own family. The irony was cruel: a life adorned with achievements had come at the cost of connection, and the accolades had left me empty. No recognition or accomplishment can fill the void of an absent presence.

Perfection, I've learned, is unattainable and unnecessary. The chipped edges, the scars, the moments you get it wrong—these are not flaws. They are your truth. They are proof that you were here, that you tried, that you dared to risk failure for the chance to grow.

THE COURAGE TO EMBRACE IMPERFECTION

If you're waiting for life to align perfectly before you begin truly living, you will wait forever. I've wasted years trying to force life into boxes it was never meant to fit, agonizing over mistakes and obsessing over flaws. It took brutal failures—broken relationships, missed opportunities, and devastating losses—to see the beauty in imperfection.

The courage to embrace imperfection is really not about giving up but truly about letting go of the need to control, the fear of judgment, and the myth of arriving at some final state of happiness. It's about surrendering to the flow of life and finding the strength to thrive in its unpredictability.

THE ENDLESS BECOMING

The greatest realization of all is this: we are never done. The journey continues—not because we are lacking but because life is infinite in its complexity and potential. The work of becoming more present, more authentic, and more whole is not a task to be completed but a dance to be embraced.

There will be more failures. There will be moments when doubt creeps in and fear whispers lies about your worth. But there will also be triumphs—small, quiet moments of grace when you feel the weight lift, when laughter fills the room, and when you look in the mirror and see not perfection but peace.

This is the paradox of life: The closer you get to the truth, the less you need to chase. The more you surrender to the flow, the more you gain. The more present you are, the more alive you feel.

KEY THEMES:

1. **Life is a Journey, Not a Finish Line:** There's no point where you suddenly "arrive" and have it all figured out. Growth is constant, and the sooner you accept that, the easier it becomes to embrace each step.
2. **Success is Built on Authenticity, Not Perfection:** The world tries to measure success in numbers, titles, and achievements, but real success comes from staying true to yourself and the connections you build along the way.
3. **Imperfection is Freedom, Not Failure:** Trying to be perfect is exhausting and impossible. Embracing your flaws and mistakes is what truly sets you free.

LESSONS AND REFLECTIONS:

1. **Growth Never Stops:** Becoming the best version of yourself isn't a one-time event—it's a process that lasts your entire life. There will always be something to learn, something to refine, and something to let go of.
2. **Being Present is More Powerful Than Any Accomplishment:** Achievements fade, but the way you show up in each moment is what really defines your life.
3. **Failure Isn't the End—It's the Start of What's Next:** Every time something doesn't go as planned, it's not a dead-end—it's just a redirect toward something new. The only real failure is refusing to keep going.

ACTIONABLE STEPS:

1. **Practice Gratitude Daily:** Reflect on three moments that brought you joy or growth, no matter how small.
2. **Set Intentions, Not Expectations:** Approach each day with a focus on how you want to show up rather than rigid goals.
3. **Forgive Yourself:** Write down one perceived failure and identify the lesson it taught you.
4. **Celebrate Small Wins:** Acknowledge your progress, even if it feels insignificant.

CONCLUSION:

Over four decades of existence, I have learned one unshakable truth: the essence of life lies in how you show up—for yourself, for others, and for the moment at hand. It is not about changing who you are but learning to embrace it, nurture it, and let it unfold.

You will rise. You will fall. And then you will rise again. This is the cycle, the rhythm, the dance of being human. Embrace it with all the grit, grace, and heart you can muster. This is your life—raw, relentless, and unapologetically yours.

CONCLUSION
A LIFE THAT ROARS IN THE INFINITE ECHOES OF THE PRESENT

Life ain't some neat, pretty tune. It's noise. It's chaos. It crashes, it breaks, it spits you out when you least expect it. There's no rhythm to follow, no conductor to guide you—just you, figuring out how to stand when the ground won't stay still. It does not know the past, nor does it care for the future. It is about what is happening now, the present. It doesn't apologize for the storms it brews, nor does it wait for us to be ready. It comes wild and unyielding like a tornado, daring us to rise and to fall, to stumble and to soar again.

This conclusion isn't a bow wrapped neatly around a package; it's a rallying cry, a reminder that your story doesn't end here. It begins anew with every breath, every decision, and every courageous step forward. It begins anew now. Every "now" you encounter is a new beginning. If you miss it, there is one right after.

THE MYTH OF ARRIVAL AND THE GLORY OF THE CLIMB

For decades, I chased the illusion of arrival, that mythical place where everything aligns, the chaos subsides, and the applause never fades. But life, in its brutal honesty, tore down that illusion. Arrival is a mirage, a fleeting moment where triumph whispers, "What's next?" Real living is in the climb, the grit under your nails as you ascend, the fire in your lungs as you push beyond your limits. It's in the falls that teach you resilience and the summits that humble you with their fleeting beauty.

You will never arrive because there is no destination. Life is an endless canvas, and the masterpiece is in the strokes, bold and hesitant, wild and deliberate. So, stop waiting. Stop planning for perfection. Embrace the imperfection of now and let it roar through you.

THE POWER OF BECOMING

The greatest lie we tell ourselves is that we must be something: successful, admired, untouchable. But the secret of life is this: we are not human beings; we are human becomings. Growth doesn't follow a timeline, and transformation isn't bound by age or circumstance.

Every failure carves a deeper well for wisdom, every heartbreak teaches you the depth of love, and every uncertainty forces you to find strength you didn't know you had. Don't waste your time chasing an image of who you think you should be. Instead, be curious about who you are and brave enough to meet who you are becoming.

THE FIERCE BALANCE OF PRESENCE AND POSSIBILITY

To live boldly is to hold two truths at once: the beauty of the moment and the promise of tomorrow. Presence is not a surrender; it's a battle cry. It demands that you face the NOW with open eyes and heart. Every breath you take is an act of defiance against the chaos of the world, a massive declaration that you will show up not perfectly but fully and intentionally.

And yet, presence isn't the enemy of ambition. You can dream while staying grounded and push forward while standing still. Life isn't a choice between the journey and the destination; it's the dance between them. So, be here fiercely. Be here wildly. And let the dreams you build today shape the tomorrows you'll inhabit.

A CALL TO LIVE LOUDLY

This is your life, unfolding, messy, and gloriously unfinished. Don't settle for whispers when you were born to roar. Don't wait for clarity when action will bring it. The world needs your fire, your vision, and your untamed, unpolished truth. It needs your mistakes, your lessons, and your moments of quiet triumph.

Be raw. Be bold. Be the voice that cuts through the noise with purpose and presence. Write your story with ink that doesn't fade, not for the applause of others but for the echo it leaves in the hearts of those who walk beside you and come after.

THE JOURNEY IS YOURS

I leave you with this truth: There is no roadmap, no secret, no end. There is only the journey, infinite in its complexity and breathtaking in its simplicity. Live it fully. Love recklessly. Fail courageously. Rise unrelentingly. This isn't goodbye. This is the beginning of your next chapter. The pen is in your hands, and the roar of life is yours to unleash.

Go live it—loudly, boldly, unapologetically.

THANK YOU FOR READING MY BOOK!

Download Your Free Gifts

Just to say thanks for buying and reading my book, I would like to give you a free welcome call with me, no strings attached!

To Download, Scan the QR Code:

I appreciate your interest in my book and value your feedback as it helps me improve future versions of this book. I would appreciate it if you could leave your invaluable review on Amazon.com with your feedback. Thank you!

www.ingramcontent.com/pod-product-compliance
Lightning Source LLC
Chambersburg PA
CBHW020248010526
44107CB00002B/149